COLONIAL EDUCATION FOR AFRICANS

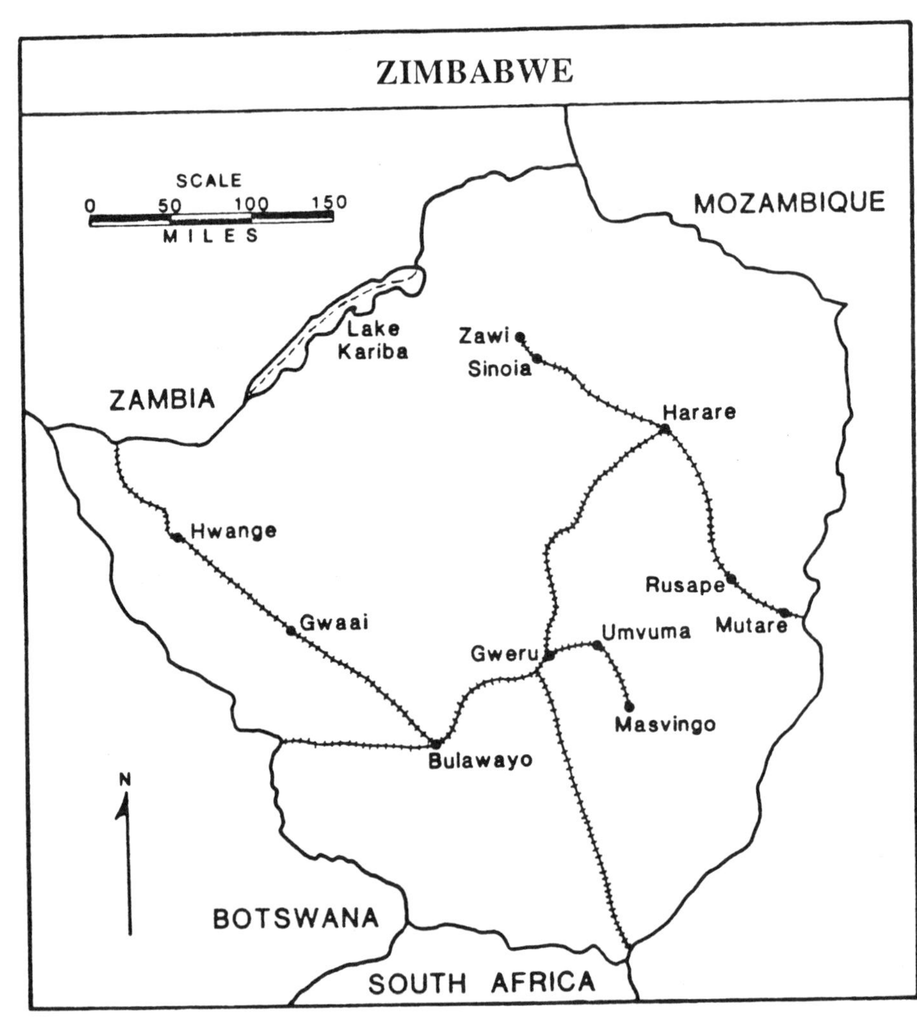
ZIMBABWE
SCALE
0
50
100
150
MILES
MOZAMBIQUE
Lake
Kariba
Zawi
Sinoia
ZAMBIA
Harare
Hwange
Rusape
Gwaai
Umvuma
Mutare
Gweru
Masvingo
Bulawayo
N
BOTSWANA
SOUTH AFRICA

COLONIAL EDUCATION FOR AFRICANS

George Stark's Policy in Zimbabwe

Dickson A. Mungazi

New York
Westport, Connecticut
London

Library of Congress Cataloging-in-Publication Data

Mungazi, Dickson A.
Colonial education for Africans : George Stark's policy in Zimbabwe / Dickson A. Mungazi.
p. cm.
Includes bibliographical references and index.
ISBN 0-275-94029-2 (alk. paper)
1. Education—Zimbabwe—History—20th century. 2. Stark, George. 3. Education—Zimbabwe—Aims and objectives. 4. Zimbabwe—Colonial influence. I. Title.
LA1591.M85 1991
370'.96891—dc20 91-2273

British Library Cataloguing in Publication Data is available.

Library of Congress Catalog Card Number: 91-2273
ISBN: 0-275-94029-2

First published in 1991

Praeger Publishers, One Madison Avenue, New York, NY 10010
An imprint of Greenwood Publishing Group, Inc.

Printed in the United States of America

The paper used in this book complies with the Permanent Paper Standard issued by the National Information Standards Organization (Z39.48-1984).

10 9 8 7 6 5 4 3 2 1

For Mildred Taylor, teacher, humanitarian, missionary, and friend, whose dedication to the advancement of the Africans makes her special.

The fundamental objective in African education must be to make an effort to bind more closely the ties between the school and tribal life.

George Stark, 1930

Contents

Photo essay follows page 57.

Preface

The purpose of this study is to furnish evidence to substantiate the following arguments: that the implementation of the policy of practical training and tribal conditioning, as defined and designed by George Stark, director of native education in colonial Zimbabwe from 1934 to 1954, had a negative effect on the educational development of Africans, that this practical training was synonymous with manual labor, underscoring the uniqueness of the objectives he sought to accomplish to train Africans to serve the interests of the colonial government and to confine them to tribal settings, that this policy left a legacy of educational underdevelopment with which post colonial Zimbabwe is now wrestling.

Two elements have been identified in this study as constituting Stark's philosophy and goals of education for Africans: to prepare them to function as efficient laborers, as ''hewers of wood and drawers of water for their white masters,'' and to confine them to tribal settings. The effect of this policy on Africans was that they were denied an effective role in the affairs of their country.

The evidence used to substantiate this conclusion comes from original materials and official documents that the author obtained while he was conducting extensive research in Zimbabwe in 1983 and 1989. In presenting this evidence, the study seeks to answer the following questions: How did Western education for Africans begin in Zimbabwe? What were the major objectives of the colonial government for the education of Africans? What was Stark's role in seeking to fulfill them? What was his philosophy of African education?

The annual reports that he wrote over two decades and other official documents and materials are the major sources for the study, and from the core of the evidence used to substantiate the author's conclusions. In presenting this evidence, the study substantiates the following conclusions: Stark's philosophy of education for Africans was heavily influenced by the conditions arising from the Victorian traditional attitudes and the desire to sustain the structure of the colonial status quo. The alliance between Stark and Godfrey Huggins, prime minister from 1933 to 1953, not only shaped their destiny and their careers but also sealed their political fate. In two decades, this alliance did more harm than good to the cause of African advancement - educational, political, and socioeconomic.

The disabilities the Africans suffered in education handicapped them in other areas of national life. The legacy of Stark's policies can still be seen in the educational problems that Zimbabwe is facing today. The interview that the author had in 1983 with Ian Smith, the last colonial prime minister, offers some insights into the character of the history of colonial educational policy and how it created problems for the future.

Acknowledgements

In the process of writing a book about the work of a highly controversial colonial leader whose term of office extended over a period of two decades, one must rely heavily on official documents and original materials, which form the core of his record. For this reason the author wishes to extend his profound gratitude to the Zimbabwe National Archives for allowing him access to original documents and official records on George Stark, George Duthie, Harold Jowitt, Herbert Keigwin, and other government officials whose record of policy he studied to produce this manuscript.

The author also wishes to thank the Old Mutare Methodist Archives and other church organizations and institutions for allowing him access to their records and documents. He wishes to extend his special gratitude to Ian Smith, the last colonial prime minister, who served from 1964 to 1979, for giving him an interview in 1983 from which he obtained some useful insights into some of the historical aspects of the colonial educational policies under Godfrey Huggins and George Stark, and how they influenced those of his own administration.

Likewise, the author wishes to thank Bishop Abel Muzorewa, founding member of the African National Council (1970) and interim prime minister (1979) as well as Rev. Ndabaningi Sithole, founding member of the African National Congress (1957) former president of the Zimbabwe African National Union (ZANU), and a member of the transitional government (1979), for granting him interviews from which he obtained valuable information regarding problems of African education during the post Stark era.

The author also wishes to thank Jill Tailey, Ed Bulinski, Betty Russell, and Marge Maston, all of the Center for Excellence in Education at Northern Arizona University, for their assistance in programming the computer so that the manuscript could be produced more efficiently, and Jerry Braun, also of Northern Arizona University, for preliminary editing of the manuscript and Linda Gregonis, indexer. In addition he wishes to thank many people, both in Zimbabwe and in the United States, especially members of the International and Comparative Education Society and the National Social Science Association, for their interest and constructive criticism offered during the time the author was presenting papers at professional conferences from 1984 to 1989.

To William and Verna Kodzai, the author wishes to express his special appreciation for their hospitality and other forms of assistance while he was in Zimbabwe in 1983 and 1989, and to Mr. Benjamin Mabvuta, senior teacher at George Stark Secondary School in Harare, for valuable information and for taking him on a tour of the school in August 1989. The author wishes to express his special gratitude to Jeanette Weatherby and Rebecca Steed both of the Faculty Services Office in the Center for Excellence in Education at Northern Arizona University for their assistance in dispatching the manuscript to the publisher and in other ways.

Finally, the author wishes to thank his family — his wife, Della, his daughter, Marcia, and his sons, Alan and Gaylord, for giving him constant support and encouragement, without which the study could not have been completed.

Introduction

The Purpose of Establishing Colonies

There is evidence to suggest that the war of independence, which placed Zimbabwe in the headlines of newspapers around the world from April 1966 to December 1979, had its origins in events that took place in earlier times. For this reason a study of any aspect of any colonial period reveals some disturbing realities that can be comprehended only in retrospect. Also for this reason, historiography becomes a powerful instrument with which to examine some of humanity's best achievements and worst moments.

Translated into implications for everyday life, this contradiction enables one to understand why, sooner or later, there is conflict between the colonial government and the colonized. It is a paradoxical reality, a sad irony, that while colonial governments find it hard to comprehend the causes of such conflicts, the colonized find them easy to grasp. One fundamental reason is that colonial governments formulate policies to ensure not the advancement of the colonized but the advancement of their own socioeconomic and political interests.

Wherever colonial governments have been established, from the Roman Empire to European colonial governments in Africa, the major objective of colonialism has been to exploit resources, both human and material, for the sole benefit of the colonizer. This is the perspective, the reality, from which this study examines the effect of the policy that George Stark formulated and pursued with regard to the educational process for Africans in colonial Zimbabwe from 1934 to 1954.

To obtain the maximum profit possible, colonial governments enact laws that are blunt in their intent and exploitive in their implementation. Among the better-known examples are the infamous corn laws that Britain enacted between 1361 and 1835 to safeguard its economic interests. The British landlords, many of them powerful members of Parliament, supported these laws because they forced the struggling people in the colonies to pay heavy fees and thus brought them to the brink of bankruptcy. The farmers who were directly affected by these laws, were also required to pay heavy rents, thus compounding their economic difficulties.

Thus, in order to continue their agricultural operations, the farmers had to charge such high prices for their produce that the burden of sustaining the economy in the colonies fell on the shoulders of the masses, who had neither political power nor any other means of alleviating the hardships imposed on them. In Africa, the proverbial white man's burden suddenly became the Africans' real economic and social burden.

As with the anti-Corn Law movement, beginning in 1830, the colonized often find ways of registering their discontent with the colonial conditions. The elements of political consciousness that come out of such situations often lead to an open struggle to end not only the conditions of hardship but also colonialism itself. The formation of the Anti-corn law League and the emergence of the theory of Adam Smith, for example, manifested the conviction that colonialism was not destined to last forever.

Although it can last as long as the colonizer is able to oppress the colonized and every colonial condition is oppressive because it is exploitive there comes a time when the colonized will rise up against colonial rule.

One recent example of colonial oppression is what *Time* (September 21, 1987) described as deplorable conditions of life to which the Australian government has reduced the Aborigines. A study of this aspect of the history of Australia will lead to the conclusion that since the British began shipping convicts there in 1788, the Aborigines have endured the agony of colonial oppression far more severely than the Australian government cares to admit. Having been moved to the fringes of society, and subjected to deprivation, bare existence, and denial of equal educational opportunity for many years, the Aborigines are now beginning to rise up against the reality of colonial oppression. This is the pattern of action that colonialism anywhere eventually evokes in the colonized.

The Purpose of Establishing Colonies in Africa

If colonial conditions were hard elsewhere, they were far more oppressive in Africa. The European nations formulated political and socioeconomic theories on which to base policies in a way that no previous colonial masters had done. The uniqueness of colonialism in Africa was caused by conditions is Europe in the nineteenth century. The Industrial Revolution altered the life-style that Europeans had known for centuries. Mechanization and the quest for material wealth combined in a powerful way to place European nations in a situation that demanded territorial expansion and, hence, colonization.

The scramble for colonies in Africa beginning in 1875, and the convening of the Berlin Conference in 1884, ushered in a new era in the history of colonization. The need for raw materials superseded every other consideration. When the brutality of slavery ended, the brutality of grand imperial designs took its place, and the vicious cycle began again. Both natural resources and the African people became the major target of European entrepreneurs. For colonialists the world of tomorrow was here and now. Individuals like Cecil John Rhodes became the majestic symbol of that British "brooding spirit" which John Stuart Mill so eloquently described. By 1900 the British influence was so vast that British nationalists and colonialists could boast that the sun never set on the British Empire. But events would later prove that for all his political power, Rhodes, like his successors, was a tragic colonial figure. While it lasted, however, colonialism in Africa provided the ultimate European frontier. Victorian Europeans had never been so well off. There was nothing greater, nothing more exciting than the feeling that they had conquered and subdued the vast "Dark Continent," and that its riches and raw materials were under their control. This is what made Rhodes one of the richest men in the world only a few years after he arrived in South Africa in 1870, enabling him to finance his expeditions into Zimbabwe as the first stage of his endeavor to bring all of Africa under the British Empire.

Along with the establishment of a vast colonial empire came what was known as colonial policy. Each European nation practiced a policy suited to its own conditions.

For example, Germany practiced deutsche Kolonialbund, Portugal practiced Estado Novo, Belgium and France implemented a policy known as evalue, and Britain practiced a policy of indirect rule. These policies had a common purpose. They were all intended to promote the interests of the colonial establishments themselves rather to advance the native people. Indeed, in Africa, any benefit that the Africans may have derived from colonialism was a result of their own effort to make the best of an exploiting system. This is true of their efforts to secure something better than the colonial governments intended for them through their educational systems.

The Rise of George Stark

The preceding account is the reality one must take into account in discussing the effect of the policy that George Stark formulated and pursued for the education of Africans in colonial Zimbabwe. But to understand why Stark pursued his policy as he did, one must first understand the conditions that produced the government he served. The signing of the Rudd Concession on October 30, 1888, which gave Rhodes exclusive mining rights; the establishment of a colonial administration in September 1890; the assassination of King Lobengula by Rhodes's agents in 1893; the introduction of the infamous Orders in Council in 1894; the naming of the country Southern Rhodesia in 1895; and the outbreak of the bitter war of resistance in 1896 were events that proved the colonialists were prepared to go to any length to subject the Africans to colonial rule and thereby ensure the full exploitation of the raw materials.

From the beginning of the administration of Leander Starr Jameson in 1890 to the end of that of Ian Smith in 1979, the colonial government pursued only one major policy toward the Africans: to educate them so that they would become efficient and economical laborers. This study will cite evidence to substantiate this conclusion. It will also show that the basis of this policy was that for the colonial entrepreneurs to make profit, they needed cheap labor. The colonial government recognized that to function as cheap laborers, the Africans had to be trained. The colonial entrepreneurs did not know that whatever form that training took, it meant an educational process whose outcome, including the rise of African consciousness, they could not predict or control. Thus, the seeds of conflict were sown.

An understanding of the conditions that produced George Stark leads one to ask three important questions: Who was George Stark? What was his mission? What was his philosophy of education for Africans? To furnish answers to these questions is to discuss the major features of his policy. In stating his philosophy of education for Africans as being based upon elements of practical training and tribal conditioning, Stark became a champion of the colonial cause. In reversing the policy that his predecessor, Harold Jowitt had formulated for the development of African education, he became an undisputed authority in a highly controversial area of national importance.

In discussing Stark's educational policy one must understand that because he was a product of Victorian conditions, he had no alternative but to design his policy as he did. But in doing so he inadvertently helped create an environment that later generated a serious conflict between the Africans and the colonial government. His policy left a legacy that, by 1960, the Africans recognized as a major handicap to their development. In his enthusiasm to design an educational policy for Africans consistent with his philosophy of tribal conditioning and practical training to prepare them to function as laborers, Stark either ignored or neglected to take a simple and basic educational principle into account: the Africans would rise above the level which they had been reduced and would translate the intellectual potential and skills they learned — to use the plumb line to build a wall, to use their knowledge of agriculture to raise crops, or to use a saw and hammer to build a chair into an understanding of the meaning of the Pythogorean theorem, the implications of Edward Gibbon's interpretation of history, or the social implications of Shakespeare's plays or the novels of Dickens. The failure of George Stark and the the colonial government to take this principle into consideration is what the Africans took into account in launching an assault on the colonial political institutions.

The Rise of Godfrey Huggins

Therefore, from the enactment of the Education Ordinance of 1899 to the New Education Policy of 1971, the Africans endured the inadequacy of an educational system which was intended to enable them to function only as cheap laborers who would enable the colonial entrepreneurs to make profit. These are the conditions under which Stark formulated his policy. The events that produced Stark were a sequel to those from which Godfrey Huggins (1883-1971) came. It is not possible to understand Stark's work without reference to Huggins.

In examining the conditions from which Huggins came, one must go back to the beginning of Western education for Africans in Zimbabwe. This entails a discussion of the work done by Christian missionaries, starting with the opening of Inyati School by Robert Moffat of the London Missionary Society in 1859, and the reasons for their endeavors, the objectives they sought to accomplish, the problems they encountered, and why the Africans responded as they did. Only then can one understand the policy Huggins and Stark formulated for the education of Africans. This is the point at which this study begins.

Godfrey Huggins was an unusual figure in the political arena of colonial Zimbabwe. Huggins's regarding his election in 1924 to the first 'responsible government' which came into being as a result of the national referendum held in 1923, as the opportunity of a lifetime helped to shape his political career for the next 32 years. In 1925, seizing the opportunity arising from the political chaos, Huggins eliminated his rival to become the leader of the Rhodesia Party.

He immediately began to formulate his political philosophy and to put in place a socioeconomic agenda based on his views of race and the Victorian perception of the place of Africans in a society controlled by the whites.

The unexpected death of Charles Coghlan (1863-1927), the first premier under the 'Responsible Government' greatly improved Huggins's political fortunes. In 1933, taking advantage of the political demise of Howard Moffat, Robert Moffat's grandson, who had served briefly as prime minister, and of George Mitchell, his successor, who also served briefly, Huggins exploited the political uncertainty and the devastation of the Great Depression to place himself in the seat of power. From that time until he retired from active politics, Huggins operated on the belief that there must be a partnership between Africans and whites in the development of the country; as late as 1952, he defined that partnership as the kind of relationship that exists "between the horse and the rider."

Having come to Zimbabwe from Britain in 1911 as a medical practitioner in search of adventure and fortune, Huggins brought his Victorian beliefs about Africans with him. When the opportunity finally came, he found a faithful ally in George Stark. Together, Huggins and Stark shaped each other's destiny. For two decades they formulated a philosophy and designed a set of educational policies with a single objective: to make Africans into cheap laborers.

The reality that one must comprehend here is that if Stark and Huggins had envisaged the inevitable transformation of Rhodesia into Zimbabwe, they would have designed a set of policies different from the one they produced. But since they had come out of the Victorian era, a vision of changed circumstances or of the future different from the past was not a hallmark of their thinking.The legacy of the Huggins-Stark policies is clearly evident in the policies of the Rhodesia Front government.

Stark's Educational Policy for Africans: Questions to Be Answered

There is no doubt that Huggins and Stark operated under the Victorian belief that Africans could benefit only from manual training as a viable form of education. The creation of the Department of Native Education in 1927, during the administration of Charles Coghlan, was intended to coordinate all efforts to ensure that Africans received an education which would prepare them to function as cheap laborers. But to understand why Huggins and Stark formulated and pursued the kind of policy they did, one needs to understand the work Harold Jowitt did from 1927 to 1934. To understand what Jowitt did, one must understand what George Duthie and Herbert Keigwin did from 1902 to 1925. Each was part of an era that began to unfold in a sequence of developments beginning with the enactment of the Education Ordinance of 1899.

Therefore, this study focuses on answering the following questions: What was the role of Western missionaries in the introduction of Western education for the Africans of Zimbabwe? Why did the colonial government enter the arena of educational policy in 1899? Who were the colonial officials who played a major role in formulating educational policy for Africans? What role did George Duthie, Herbert Keigwin, and Harold Jowitt play in laying the foundation on which Stark built his policy? Why did Stark formulate his policy for African education as he did? What effect did implementing that policy have on the education of Africans? What was the legacy of his policy?

Stark's work was part of a coordinated complex of the Victorian legacy and of ideals formulated by successive colonial administrations to strengthen it. The colonial government never wavered in its belief that the education of Africans must prepare them to be efficient "drawers of water and hewers of wood for their white masters," although with the passage of time it acquired more subtle techniques to conceal its intent.

A tragic feature of the colonial officials who came out of the Victorian period is that the Industrial Revolution severely limited their ability to view people of other races, especially Africans, as distinctive products of the environment or social conditions under which they lived. Failure to consider all relevant factors in assessing the potential of Africans had reduced the members of the colonial hierarchy to the point where they, like the machines invented by European entrepreneurs behaved in mechanical fashion. In this manner they created stereotypes that controlled their thinking, their policies, and their behavior toward Africans. Having created an environment that was less than adequate, concluded that Africans lacked intellectual potential and, therefore must be treated as less intelligent than the whites.

Reduced to their simple and basic application, both the Victorian traditions and the Industrial Revolution placed whites in a situation from which they could not extricate themselves. The tragedy of this thinking found its greatest expression in the founding of colonies in Africa. In Zimbabwe, as elsewhere in Africa, racial discrimination, economic deprivation of the African masses, and exploitation of resources, both human and material, accentuated the negative rather than the positive, the bad rather than the good. Both the colonial officials and the Africans were the ultimate casualties of a set of policies designed to promote the political and socioeconomic interests of the whites. This study shows how Stark became its ultimate victim.

The Legacy of Stark's Educational Policy

In a real sense, therefore, post colonial Zimbabwe is still paying the price of the tragedy of the Higgins-Stark era. Poverty, illiteracy, disease, and political dissent have taken a heavy toll, and will take long time to overcome. In Africa as a whole, most governments have already given up the struggle. The task is too formidable for them, the costs so prohibitive that it is not worth the effort. Colonialism has forced African nations to depend on Western capital and technology once more. There is no escape from the vicious tentacles of an old octopus. In 1983, Ian Smith told the author that the educational policy of his government was a legacy of the policy pursued by previous administrations, and that it was not realistic to expect his government to break away from policies that had been pursued in the past.

Indeed, in Zimbabwe this situation is directly related to the policies that George Stark pursued. The legacy he created did not suddenly disappear with his political demise in 1954, or with the end, in 1979, of the colonial condition he helped to strengthen with an inadequate educational policy. Rather, Zimbabwe is faced with new and challenging political and socioeconomic problems of immense proportions. A senior teacher at George Stark Secondary School in Harare (opened in 1955 as a primary school) told the author during a visit to the school on August 2, 1989,

> A few years ago, the white headmaster of the school pulled down the framed photograph of George Stark from a prominent position it had been hanging in the school, removed it from the frame, and pinned it on a bulletin board in an obscure room. This pseudo white Zimbabwean nationalist then argued that the educational policy that Stark pursued contributed greatly to the problems that we are now facing in this country.

The knowledge of the strategy which Stark used will undoubtedly help in overcoming these problems.

A thriving and dynamic young nation, Zimbabwe has been recognized as having a potential for greatness unequaled by any other country in Africa. But it will need to guard its resources, both human and material, and to educate its people in a manner which will elevate that potential to a new level of national development and, thus, to greatness. The policies that Stark and Huggins pursued relative to the education of Africans are not distant or remote phases of colonial history, but are part and parcel of the legacy and the problems that Zimbabwe must now learn to resolve. The task is not an easy one, but it can be accomplished in a manner that translates into national prosperity.

Some Facts About Zimbabwe (1940)

1. Date of colonization	September 1890
2. Colonizing nation	Great Britain
3. Area	150,333 square miles
4. Population	3.1 million Africans 123,000 whites
5. Annual population growth rate	2.7%
6. Literacy	21.0% Africans 79.0% whites
7. Annual per capita income	$3,000 whites $48.00 Africans
8. Total amount spent on education	$7.3 million for whites $204,212 for Africans
9. Leading towns	Salisbury (Harare), Bulawayo, Mutare, Gweru, Kadoma
10. Leading industries	Mining, agriculture
11. Form of government	Parliament of 30 white members elected by white voters
12. Leader of the government	Godfrey Huggins (1933-1952)

1
The Meaning of the Introduction of Western Education for Africans in Zimbabwe

We do not intend to hand over this country to the Natives. Let us make no pretense of educating them in the same way we educate Whites.

—*Tawse Jollie, during a debate in the legislature, 1927*

The Purpose of This Study

The purpose of this study is to discuss how the educational philosophy that George Stark, director of native education in colonial Zimbabwe from 1933 to 1954, formulated for the education of Africans combined with a set of policies he designed to effect their development. Because Stark was a product of the Victorian perception of Africans, it would not be realistic to expect him to design policies involving the development of Africans outside the confines of that perception.

Important questions that the study seeks to answer include the following: Who was George Stark? What considerations did he take into account in formulating his philosophy and designing his policy for the education of Africans? What conditions influenced his task? Who were some of the people with whom he worked? How did Africans respond to his policy? What legacy did the implementation of his policy leave for post colonial Zimbabwe? In order to appreciate why Stark formulated his policy as he did, we must first discuss the meaning of the introduction of Western education for Africans in Zimbabwe.

To understand why Stark formulated his policy the way he did demands a discussion of the role of Christian missionaries because, at its inception, the educational process, both for Africans and for whites, was the responsibility of church organizations. Because church organizations were themselves a product of Western culture, the educational process they introduced acquired the characteristics of Western culture in an African cultural settings.

The Role of Christian Missionaries in Perspective

When Robert Moffat of the London Missionary Society opened the first school for Africans at Inyati in 1859, neither he nor the Africans were aware that in introducing Western education, the whites, both missionaries and lay persons, intended to pursue a set of objectives designed to promote their own interests. Therefore, from its inception, Western education acquired political dimensions that would affect Africans in profound ways. The Christian missionaries, in the forefront of introducing Western education to the Africans of Zimbabwe, did not negate the fact that they were seeking to promote their own interests. In time Christianity as a basis of new cultural relationships became a potent factor of controlling Africans in a new religious environment.

Encouraged by the modest success of his efforts, Moffat sought and secured the permission of the skeptical King Mzilikazi to open a second school at Hope Fountain in 1870. From that time until 1893, other Christian bodies, both Catholic and Protestant, opened schools for Africans in various parts of the country for the purpose of promoting Christianity and, hence, transforming the life-style of the Africans.[1]

The introduction of Western education to the Africans of Zimbabwe by Christians was poised to change permanently the way of life that Africans had known for hundreds of years. Because the education of Africans remained largely the responsibility of Christian organizations until the church-state crisis of 1969, it stressed the learning of moral and religious values as the most important objective.[2] When applied to conditions of human existence in Africa, especially under colonial rule, the Bible carried an explicit message of obedience that became an instrument of control. In the context of colonial conditions, that control became synonymous with oppression.

The opening of schools for Africans was a product of the Victorian enthusiasm among Western Christian missionaries to promote Christianity as the most important means of ensuring their advancement. Among the most ardent Christian enthusiasts was David Livingstone (1813-1873), who, like Moffat, carried out his missionary work under the sponsorship of the London Missionary Society.

History has portrayed and glamorized Livingstone as a dedicated missionary who had a vision of Africa and of the life and culture of its people radically transformed by Christian values and European culture. But the contradiction in the behavior of whites in the context of their culture and civilization is evinced in the fact that upon his arrival in southern Africa in 1841, Livingstone launched a crusade not against the presumed primitive African culture but against the evils of slavery, the product of his own civilization, as the first priority of his missionary career. But in his dedication and attempts to help Europeans accept Africans into the Christian circle during the height of the age of imperialism, Livingstone appears to have been fighting for a lost cause. Conditions forced him to make some adjustment and to compromise the principles he thought were essential to the success of his missionary endeavors.

What is even more important about the introduction of the Western concept of material wealth is that it had become a new, potent force for controlling Africans beyond the level the entrepreneurs had envisaged. During the twentieth century the concept of material wealth translated into an economic power that the colonial governments used to control the Africans effectively. Therefore, government control of education added a new dimension to introducing Western education for Africans.

With the advent of the Industrial Revolution, the Christian message that Livingstone and other Western missionaries were attempting to persuade the Africans to accept seems to have been lost in the confusion and conflict that emerged between religious values and the search for material comfort as a demonstration of the distinctive British entrepreneurial ingenuity. It became a victim of the materialism and commercial entrepreneurial adventure that even the most ardent missionaries found hard to resist. Material comfort, as the intended outcome of the Industrial Revolution, combined with the British 'brooding spirit,' which John Stuart Mill so eloquently described, to compel the missionaries to alter their objective from promoting Christianity to promoting European commercial interests as a specific element of exercising control over the Africans. Livingstone, speaking at Oxford University in 1864, went to great lengths to explain why he and his missionary colleagues were reversing their objectives:

> Sending the Gospel to the heathens of Africa must include much more than is implied in the usual practice of a missionary, namely a man going about with a Bible under his arms. The promotion of commerce ought to be specially attended to as this, more than anything else, makes the heathen tribes depend on commercial intercourse among civilized nations. I go back to open a new path to commerce, do you carry on the work I have begun?[3]

Therefore, the Africans' image of Livingstone as a missionary motivated by a religious objective of promoting their advancement through education was replaced by a new image of him as a fervent Scottish nationalist motivated by the objective of promoting British commercial interests. The commercial vehicle that the European entrepreneurs were now trying to build with fervent determination was intended to run on the social and political wheels of Western cultural values, propelled by the engine of economic prosperity and fueled by cheap labor. This is the reason why, from the 1865 to 1899, the sole purpose of the Western Christian missionary educational effort among Africans was the promotion of British commercial interests and conversion to Christianity as a means of having them accept British cultural influence and political power. But between 1880 and 1896, the elements of conflict between the missionaries and the colonialists became apparent when the former emphasized religious instruction and the latter emphasized manual labor as a more appropriate form of education for Africans.

The change of missionary objective from establishing Christianity in Africa to promoting Western commercial interests was a development that had a negative influence on Africans' response to the message the missionaries were trying to persuade them to accept. Thus, in 1882, six years before the Rudd Concession, by which Cecil John Rhodes claimed to have the permission of King Lobengula to establish mining operations in Zimbabwe, Moffat expressed his disappointment with his failure to persuade the Africans to accept Christianity:

> A few individuals may have been influenced for good, but there is no organic result. There does not seem to be two people of the tribe who recognize each other as Christians. There is no indication that life in the tribe is in any way touched by the Gospel.[4]

For all his missionary enthusiasm, Moffat appears to have lost touch with the real cause of African negative response: contradiction in the behavior of the missionaries and the extent of control they wished to exercise over the African mind through religious instruction.

From all this, one is led to the conclusion that the acquiescence of the Victorian Christian missionaries to British colonial objectives resulted in a partnership between the colonial government and the church in promoting British commercial interests through the introduction of Western education for Africans in order to control them.

While this may not have been the intention of the missionaries, it certainly was the effect of their action on the attitudes of Western entrepreneurs toward the Africans.

The question now arises: If Christian missionaries wanted Western education to help Africans accept Christianity, on the assumption that it meant their own advancement, why did they not succeed in convincing Africans that accepting Christianity would, in effect, be good for them? The answer lies in the Africans' perception of the value of Christianity as a distinctive product of Western culture that colonialists used to control them and promote their own interests.

Therefore, the introduction of Christianity and Western education for the Africans of Zimbabwe meant, in effect, the introduction of Western culture with all the negative things they believed it entailed. Viewed from the Victorian perspective, therefore, for the Africans to accept Western education, they had to accept Christianity and the world of the white man's culture first. That this was not easy is shown by their negative response. Nevertheless, from 1859 to 1899, the missionaries' educational activity among the Africans set the stage for major developments, especially those of the colonial government.

Controversy Between Church and State over African Education

The establishment of the colonial government in September 1890 ushered in conditions the Christian missionaries had not foreseen. There is no doubt that the colonial government was pleased with the change of missionary objective, as Livingstone had outlined in his address at Oxford University in 1864. But it was unhappy because the essential goal of missionary education was "to stabilize the faith of converts and assist in character development,"[5] instead of preparing them to contribute to the promotion of British commercial activity. This difference of opinion regarding the proper educational objective for Africans was as cruel as it was damaging to their educational development. That this difference was slowly but steadily leading to a major institutional controversy about the place of Africans in the colonial society as an outcome of the kind of education provided them by the white government is evident in the events that followed. The education of Africans became a subject of debate among colonial officials and church leaders following the bitter war of 1896-1897 is not because it was in the hands of missionaries but because of what it was designed to do.

The conflicting viewpoints that various segments of the white community were expressing by 1898 about what that education should be, demonstrate how controversial the education of Africans would become. From its very beginning, the education of Africans acquired powerful socioeconomic dimensions determined by those who were sensitive to its implications for the future. The reality of this situation is that, having come out of slavery and a devastating war in 1896-1897 the Africans believed that the colonial officials wanted that education so controlled that it would not enable them to acquire the capacity for critical thinking.

The question at the center of this debate was: What kind of education should the Africans receive? The answer determined who should control that education. That the colonial officials and the missionaries had conflicting ideas about the answer suggests how critically important it was to furnish a clear answer. But a clear answer was possible only if the two sides agreed, and they did not. The missionaries argued that the education of Africans must include literacy and religious instruction. But the colonial officials wanted only an education that would produce cheap laborers.

Among the colonial officials who felt compelled to contribute to this unprecedented debate was Earl Grey (1851-1917), who served as administrator from April 12, 1896, to December 4, 1898. With a sense of duty required by the high office he held, and conscious of the future implications of finding an answer to the question of what constituted good education for Africans and who should control it, Grey vigorously argued that the government must control Africans' education because it had the responsibility to design a policy for national development.

In 1898, when he introduced the first bill on education, Grey argued "I am convinced that the very first step towards civilizing the Natives lies in a course of industrial and practical training which must precede the teaching of [religious] dogma."[6] Grey was quite candid in defining "industrial training" as being synonymous with manual labor. This is exactly what the education ordinance that the British South Africa Company legislature enacted in 1899 was intended to accomplish.

The reality of the growing institutional controversy over the main objective of African education and who should control it is revealed in the views that Reverend Arthur Bathe expressed in opposition to Grey, saying: "I am sorry that on the part of the whites there is a reluctance to encourage good education among the Natives under the pretext that they will not be useful as cheap laborers when they can read and write."[7]

It is clear that Bathe knew that what Grey and William Milton, his successor, defined as industrial training was nothing more more training the Africans as laborers. What troubled the missionaries about the definition of the colonial government relative to the character of education for Africans was not that it had moved to have its own policies prevail at the expense of the missionaries', but that in formulating such policies it would render the religious values of the educational process meaningless through the emergence of a totally secular educational system.

Two observations must be made at this point regarding the controversy about the educational objectives in African education. The first is that the Victorian missionaries readily recognized that if the views of the colonial officials about the character of education for Africans prevailed, the resulting educational process would reduce their influence in the life of the people whom they believed only they could change for the good. Their learning this was a painful experience that caused them to wonder if they had lost the major objective of their work.

The second observation is that for the missionaries to regard African traditional religion as primitive, to expect the Africans to discard the customs of their ancestors during a period when the memories of the bitter war of 1896-1897 were still fresh in their minds, was to expect them to discard their cultural identity and religious practices. The whites' negative attitude toward the essentials of African culture did not help their cause.

Therefore, from the time Livingstone endorsed the general goal of colonial activity in 1864 to the time that the colonial government enacted the first legislation on education in 1899, the missionaries alienated themselves from the Africans, losing the influence they should have exerted. Only after they realized their influence had been damaged did they begin to question the policies of the colonial government by critically appraising their own.

Geoffrey Kapenzi, a Zimbabwean theologian, explains how the thinking among missionaries was detrimental to their cause and how they were losing the struggle for control of the education of Africans:

> The vast majority of the missionaries referred to the Africans as the degraded descendants of Ham and as Kaffir Natives. Therefore, the missionaries did not practice Biblical Christianity, but colonial religion in which African-missionary relations were set in their colonial pattern of masters and servants, superiors and inferiors.[8]

This observation is an accurate assessment of the views that Livingstone expressed on this matter when he wrote, ''True, the African, when Christianized, is not so elevated as we who have had the advantage of civilization and Christianity for ages.''[9]

An intriguing aspect of the Victorian missionaries is the extent of the contradiction manifested through their actions. On the one hand, they feared that if the colonial policy prevailed, they would lose the influence they thought they should exert on the conduct of education for Africans. On the other hand, they believed that before the educational process began, the Africans must show their willingness to accept Christianity. By failing to recognize that the educational process itself would bring about a change in the life of the Africans that would mean acceptance of Christianity, they closed any meaningful channels of communication between themselves and the Africans. There is no question that the colonial government took advantage of this situation to strengthen its own position.

The Effect of Legislation on African Education: The Beginning of Government Control

These developments constituted the beginning of government control of education. In 1899, aware that it had an advantage over the missionaries, the colonial government acted to implement its own educational objectives. The enactment of the first legislation for education[10] in that year gave the colonial government power to formulate its philosophy of education based on its objective of training Africans to make a contribution to the economic development of the country by functioning as laborers.

Because this legislation gave the colonial government the power it had not have since its inception in 1890, it asserted its authority by introducing the policy of industrial training for Africans. Aware that the type of education which would emerge as a result of formulating a policy and regulations requiring industrial training for Africans, the colonial government first under Grey, and then under William Milton, pushed the bill through the legislature.

Although the primary purpose of the Education Ordinance of 1899 was to assist the development of a complete academic education for white students, its impact was greater on the government power to formulate an educational policy consistent with its objectives for Africans. The main provision of this legislation, in addition to the general educational grant of $4.00 per white student who met an academic standard of proficiency in English, Latin, literature, history, mathematics, geography, science, music, and shorthand,[11] was government control. All the missionaries could do was hope that their influence on the conduct of African education did not erode totally.

There is no question that from the beginning of its direct involvement in the educational process, the government wanted to use the financial power of this legislation to ensure that the subjects listed above formed the core of the curriculum for white students, thereby ensuring that they were adequately prepared to exercise political control over the Africans.

It was, therefore, by design that Section B of this ordinance made provision for the African schools, all of them run by missionary organizations, to receive grants of ten shillings ($1.00) per student per academic year. Each school must offer no less than two hours per day of practical training and of manual labor, and must have been a total of four hours , and the average daily attendance not less than 50 during the preceding school year of 200 days.[12]

There is no doubt that the government believed it had found a workable solution to the problem it had faced since it took office in 1890. The confused state in which missionary educational policy found itself was a blessing. Now that the government had finally made its move, was the future going to be what Cecil Rhodes, Leander Starr Jameson, Earl Grey, and William Milton had predicted, or was this the opening of a new chapter in the brutal struggle ahead? It remained to be seen. The euphoria that characterized the reaction of the colonialists could be understood only in terms of what they hoped the new legislation would help to accomplish: to prepare Africans to function as cheap laborers.

The racially discriminatory character of the educational policy that came into being with the Education Ordinance of 1899 remained a standard feature throughout the rest of the colonial rule of Zimbabwe. Once the colonial government tasted the fruit of this bias against genuine development of the education of Africans, it would never give it up or change it in any way that represented a departure from the need for cheap labor. The figures below show how expenditure for education placed African students at a financial disadvantage.

Government Expenditure For White Education And For African Education Compared

Year	Expenditure for White education Amount	% of Total	Expenditure for African education Amount	% of Total	Grand Total
1909	$ 1,048,052	99.72	$ 3,000	0.28	$ 1,051,052
1919	1,855,300	98.83	22,000	1.17	1,877,300
1929	4,587,032	97.01	141,740	2.99	4,728,772
1939	7,354,208	97.30	204,212	2.70	7,558,420
1949	32,361,140	96.49	1,178,524	3.51	33,539,664

Source: *Zimbabwe Statistical Year Book, 1983.*

From the Education Ordinance of 1899 two things are clearly distinguishable. The first is that the colonial government, through its regulations, placed more restrictions on the education of Africans than it did on that of white students. While it required schools for white students to show evidence of academic performance as a condition of receiving grants, it specified that African schools must offer rigorous manual training as a condition of receiving financial aid. This action was quite compatible with the Victorian view that the Africans must be trained to function only as cheap laborers.

The second thing is that by instituting racism in the educational process, the government put in place an effective strategy to exercise power to design educational policies for Africans different from those for white education. The effect of this discrimination is that while the education of whites steadily improved, that of Africans remained essentially underdeveloped until the advent of a black majority government in 1980.

The enactment of Education Ordinance of 1899 had other effects on the character of African education. Having tasted power it had not had before, the government amended this ordinance in 1903 to add more conditions for grants to African schools. These included the requirement that there must be at least 40 students attending for 150 days, with 4 hours of manual labor per day as the core of the curriculum. In addition, the African students must be taught the basic elements of English, to help them understand instructions given by their employers, as well as habits of cleanliness and discipline.[13]

The colonial government's pleasure with this amendment is evidenced by a high-ranking official who took it upon himself to write to the editor of *The Rhodesia Herald,* a daily paper to say: "The black peril will only become a reality when the results of a misguided system of education has [sic.] taken root and the veneer of European civilization struggles with the innate savage nature of the African."[14]

It is evident that the power the government gave itself through the Education Ordinances of 1899 and 1903 was having a profound impact on its desire to design educational policy. This meant that the education of Africans, unable to develop along viable and dynamic academic lines, became nothing more than the manual labor and practical training that Grey and Milton had defined in 1898.

Among the evidence to substantiate this conclusion is that in 1904, the chief native commissioner for Matabeleland, a high-ranking official within the hierarchy of the colonial structure, argued: "The Native in his ignorance almost invariably abuses a purely bookish education, utilizing it only as means of defying authority. A purely literary education for Natives should not be considered for many years to come."[15]

This opinion reflected official government policy and strategy. The commissioner's counterpart in Mashonaland went further in outlining the principles that, he argued, must guide the government in formulating an educational policy for the Africans, saying,

> It is cheap labor that we need in this country, and it has yet to be proved that the Native who can read and write turns out [to be] a good laborer. As far as we can determine, the Native who can read and write will not work on farms and in mines. The official policy is to develop the Natives on lines least likely to lead to any risk of clashing with Europeans.[16]

Therefore, one can conclude that even basic literacy was discouraged for Africans because it was believed to enable them to become aware of the oppressive conditions under which they lived.

Unable to recognize that it was reducing the education of Africans to a level where the educational process had no meaning except to provide cheap labor, the government amended the Education Ordinance of 1903 with Ordinance Number 133 of 1907, which required that manual labor and practical training form a major component of the curriculum in all African schools, whether or not they qualified for aid grants.[17]

Colonial Educational Policy for Africans: Educating Hewers of Wood and Drawers of Water

Only a few months after the enactment of Ordinance Number 133, the government concluded that the power it had acquired was being threatened by the formation of the Southern Rhodesia Christian Conference, which came into being in 1906 and by 1907 was questioning educational policy toward the Africans. The formation of the Christian Conference reopened the debate between church and state about who must control African education.

In its first annual report in 1907, the Christian Conference expressed regret at government pursuit of a policy it believed was having an adverse effect on the course of African advancement.[18] The colonial government then initiated a process of redefining its policy in a way that seemed to address the concerns the missionaries were expressing. One such action was the naming of the Graham Commission in 1910 to investigate the character of African education. In addition to recommending that African education follow three basic lines — literacy, religion, and practical training — the commission recommended that the missionaries should be allowed to operate these schools. It added, "All schools for the instruction of Natives, whether in matters literary, or industrial, must come under the control of the government."[19]

The quality of African education, through the enactment of the Education Ordinance of 1899 and its subsequent amendments, was severely lessened. It is evident that the colonial government wanted to exercise greater control over it in the future than it had done in the past. As events began to move rapidly in this direction, the situation became more complicated. On July 19, 1912, wishing to implement the major recommendation of the Graham Commission, the colonial government enacted Ordinance Number 7 for the purpose of providing for more effective control of African schools. Paragraph 5 of this ordinance states, "The Director of Education may order the closure of any Native school if he is not satisfied as to the manner in which it is conducted."[20]

It is clear that the government was really not interested in any other form of education for Africans except manual labor and practical training. In a fashion that was typical of the attitude of the colonial government, one official explained the reason for this policy as a means of controlling the education of the Africans: "I do not consider it right that we should educate the Native in any way that will unfit him for service. The Native is and should always be the hewer of wood and the drawer of water for his white master."[21]

The criticism made by the Christian Conference — that the government requirement that African schools focus on manual labor was converting the Africans into hired slaves,[22] — was substantiated by other organizations. For example, in 1913, the Rolin Report graphically described the extent to which government obsession with labor supply had created a situation of misery for the Africans. When Henri Rolin reported, "A white trader will not hesitate to tell you that an African is a stupid animal,"[23] the true intent of the policy of industrial training and manual labor as a form of education for the Africans became fully understood for what it was.

As public opinion, both in Britain and in Zimbabwe, seemed to oppose the government policy on the education of Africans, there was a new twist in the growing conflict. The government decided to divert attention from things educational to things political. For the next ten years everything else was left in abeyance as the government, with the support of the white entrepreneurs who were harvesting huge economic and political profit from the policy of practical training and cheap labor, directed all its efforts toward negotiations with the British government on its political future. What emerged in 1923 was a new constitutional arrangement that brought a change of status from British South Africa Company rule to what was known in British colonial traditions as "responsible government." But the Christian Conference, struggling to influence the life of Africans thorough education, did not regard the government policy as responsible.

However, these developments gave the government a greater degree of freedom than it had enjoyed in the past to do as it saw fit in all its internal affairs. But the status of "responsible government" had nothing to do with the behavior of the government itself, which, instead of acting responsibly, acted in a way that proved its intent had been to place Africans in a situation from which they would never be able to rise again, as they had in 1896-1897, to threaten the political power of the whites. Therefore, as the new legislature was seated in 1924, the controversy surrounding the question of who must control African education intensified. A new dimension was introduced: The question was not only what kind of curriculum must be taught in African schools as defined by the Graham Commission of 1911, but who should control it.

When this continuing controversy forced government officials to conclude that the missionaries were no longer faithful to the spirit of institutional cooperation in the conduct of African education that had existed from the time of David Livingstone and Robert Moffat, they felt a compelling need to reaffirm a major recommendation of the Graham Commission : that the government should control African education. When the Graham Commission suggested that "Officials who directly control the Native population must be authorized and required to preach the doctrine of labor as a civilizing factor,"[24] it left no room for any other form of education. This was the argument the government used to justify its policy.

The evidence leads to the conclusion that the colonial government and the white community feared the academic educational development of Africans more than they feared anything else in their relationship with them. Reminding the members of the white community about the importance of the conclusion of the Graham Commission Ethel Tawse Jollie, one of the first women to sit in a colonial legislature, argued during a debate in 1927: "We do not intend to hand over this country to the Natives, or to admit them to the same social or political position as we ourselves are enjoying. Let us therefore make no pretense of educating them in the same way as we educate whites."[25] In his support of Jollie's argument and motion, Hugh Williams went a step further, arguing that the schools the missionaries were opening for Africans were detrimental to the future political interests of the whites. Williams had a suggestion for a solution to this growing problem: "If we clear out every school and stop all this fostering of education and development for Natives, we would much sooner become an asset to the [British] Empire."[26]

Jollie and Williams had similar ideas of controlling African education. Regardless of this negative attitude among government officials toward the educational development of Africans, two developments occurred in 1927 that had a profound effect on the future course of African education. The first was the report of the Hadfield Commission, which recommended that the 16 denominations operating schools for Africans coordinate their efforts in order to formulate common educational objectives and curriculum.[27] The commission stated that this was the best way to improve African education, which must include other components besides manual labor and practical training.

The second development in 1927 was the establishment of the Department of Native Development with Harold Jowitt as its director. Two considerations were central to this development: the government wanted to convince the missionaries that it was genuinely interested in the educational development of the Africans, and its principal objective was to have Jowitt coordinate all programs having to do with African education. For seven years Jowitt operated under a philosophy of education for Africans different from what the government wanted, a shattering experience for him. This is the subject of our discussion in Chapter 2.

Summary and Conclusion

What we have discussed in this chapter leads to two conclusions regarding the introduction of Western education for the Africans of Zimbabwe, especially developments from 1859 to 1927. The first is that the action of the missionaries in cooperating fully with the entrepreneurs later played into the hands of government officials who were ready to exploit the situation to control African education for their own political advantage. By 1899 the government felt so secure that it ventured into a new area, legislation on education, giving itself more power to control the character of African education in such a manner that it produced cheap laborers. Once this policy was put in place, the colonial government was not about to reconsider it. Rather, it strengthened it because colonial conditions survive on the denial of equal opportunity to the colonized. Thus, from 1899 to 1927, the educational opportunity for Africans was so controlled that there was no measured development.

The second conclusion is that whatever reasons it advanced for urging practical training and manual labor as viable forms of education for Africans, the real reason was that the government feared that a good academic education would enable Africans to acquire the essential elements of critical thinking, thereby enabling them to question the structure of colonial society. Tawse Jollie and Hugh Williams, as well as a host of other colonial officials, were quite candid in expressing this fear. These are among the realities and conditions that influenced the philosophy George Stark formulated and the policy he designed for the education of Africans. To understand the implications of Stark's policy, we must first discuss the effect of the policy that his predecessor, Harold Jowitt, designed and implemented.

Notes

1. For the names of these bodies, see Southern Rhodesia: The Report of the Commission of Inquiry into Native Education Alexander Kerr, Chairman, (1951), p. 3.
2. Harold Jowitt, "The Reconstruction of African Education in Rhodesia," (master's thesis, University of Cape Town, 1927), p. 4. Jowitt was appointed director of native education in colonial Zimbabwe in 1927. See Chapter 2 of this volume for his contribution to the development of African education during his term of office.
3. David Livingstone, Missionary Travels in Southern Africa, 1857-1870. Vol. II, London: Murray, 1952.
4. G. C. Grave, The Planting of Christianity in Africa:, Vol. II , London: Murray, 1954.
5. Harold Jowitt, "The Reconstruction of African Education," p. 5.
6. British South Africa Company, Record: Earl Grey, GR:1/1/11:Fols. 5474-8. Zimbabwe National Archives.
7. Robert John Challiss, "The Education Policy of the British South Africa Company in Southern Rhodesia, 1899-1904," (masters' thesis, University of Cape Town, 1968), p. 43.
8. Geoffrey Kapenzi, A Clash of Cultures: Christian Missionaries and the Shona of Rhodesia. (Washington, D.C:. University Press of America, 1978), p. 21.
9. William Monk [ed.], Dr Livingstone's Cambridge Lectures.(London: Bull and Daldy, 1960), p. 166.
10. Southern Rhodesia, Ordinance Number 18 of 1899: The Appointment of Inspector of Schools, Otherwise known as the Education Ordinance of 1899.
11. Ibid., Section A
12. Ibid. , Section B
13. Southern Rhodesia, Ordinance Number 1, 1903, Sect. D: "Schools for Natives."
14. The Rhodesia Herald, April 4, 1903.
15. Southern Rhodesia, The Annual Report of the Chief Native Commissioner for Matabeleland, 1904. In the Zimbabwe National Archives.
16. Southern Rhodesia, The Annual Report of the Chief Native Commissioner for Mashonaland, 1905. Inf the Zimbabwe National Archives.
17. Southern Rhodesia, Ordinance Number 133: Education Ordinance of 1907, Set. D. In f the Zimbabwe National Archives.
18. The Southern Rhodesia Christian Conference, Annual Report, 1907.
19. Southern Rhodesia, The Report of The Commission of Inquiry into Native Education [James Graham, Chairman], 1911, p. 15. By courtesy of the Zimbabwe National Archives.
20. Southern Rhodesia, Ordinance Number 7: Ordinance to Provide for the Control of Native Schools, July 19, 1912. In the Zimbabwe National Archives. See Chapter VII of this study for further reference to this ordinance.
21. A letter written by a reader addressed to the editor of The Rhodesia Herald, June 28, 1912.
22. Southern Rhodesia Christian Conference, Annual Report, 1912.
23. Henri Rolin, Les Lois et l'Administration de la Rhodesie. Bruxelles:l'Etablisesment Emil Bruyant, 1913.
24. The Report of The Graham Commission, Para. 40, p. 7.
25. Southern Rhodesia: Legislative Debates, 1927.
26. Ibid.
27. Southern Rhodesia, The Report of the Commission of Inquiry into Native Education, F.L. Hadfield, Chairman, 1927, para. 26, p. 7.

2
The Legacy of Duthie, Keigwin, and Jowitt: Decrying the Policy of Practical Training as an Impertinence

The Africans must not be trained to function as better hewers of wood and drawers of water for their white masters. — Harold Jowitt, 1928.

A school which is unrelated to the world in which students live is an impertinence. — Harold Jowitt, 1934.

Duthie's Opposition to the Policy of Practical Training

The question posed in Chapter 1 — how did George Stark fit into the structure of the educational policy that the colonial government designed under the Department of Native Development? — must be answered by discussing the work of his three predecessors: George Duthie, Herbert Keigwin, and Harold Jowitt.

An important provision of the Education Ordinance of 1899 was the appointment of inspector of schools. On November 26, 1901, George Duthie, the inspector appointed under this provision, visited St. Augustine's School for Africans near Penhalonga to determine if, indeed, it was carrying out its educational programs in accordance with the requirements defined by Section B of the ordinance. In a report that he submitted a few days later, Duthie expressed his apparent satisfaction with the school's effort to implement fully the policy of industrial training:

> This school devotes a greater part of its time to agricultural and other various forms of industry. I was pleased to observe that the boys were working steadily without supervision. I have no doubt that such a school as this will be a great benefit to the country. I therefore recommend a grant of twenty pounds [$40.00] for the current year to be paid immediately for the period April 1 to December 31. If there is a development of any other industry, so much the better.[1]

One reaches two conclusions from what Duthie said in this inspection report. The first is that the educational process for the Africans focused on industrial training and manual labor, as demanded by the Education Ordinance of 1899. Duthie made no mention of the desirability of academic education. The second conclusion is that Duthie had to carry out his duty in accordance with the requirements of the ordinance, whether or not he believed that the educational process he was appointed to supervise as inspector of schools was appropriate to the development of Africans. Therefore, in saying that the educational program at St. Augustine's School would be beneficial to the country, Duthie was saying what his superiors in the colonial government wanted to hear: that the Africans must be trained to function as cheap laborers. But, as a matter of principle, Duthie did not share this view.

This situation shows not only that the colonial government was pleased with the effect of its policy, but also that this was an educational program for Africans in the future. By the end of the school year 1901, the government had paid a total of $638.40 to three schools with a total enrollment of 265 students which suggests how much it wanted the African schools to produce cheap laborers. The missionaries, who operated all the schools for Africans, felt compelled to accept and implement this policy in order to influence African development along the principles they had defined since Robert Moffat of the London Missionary Society opened the first school for Africans at Inyati in 1859. But in accepting this policy as it was designed by the government, the missionaries created problems for themselves in the future.

Here is another example of how the missionaries implemented the new policy in order to qualify for aid grants. The superintendent of instruction at Old Mutare Methodist School expressed in his annual report his appreciation for what he believed to be a progressive policy: "The existence of this school today is sufficient proof that the requirements laid down by the British South Africa Company to engage the Natives in a course of practical training have been fully met."[2] However, events began to change the opinion of some individuals directly related to the conduct of African education. In less than four years, Duthie, who appeared to have been quite enthusiastic about playing a critical role in supervising the implementation of the policy of practical training, came to recognize its long-term harmful effects. That the enthusiasm he had previously shown in supporting the policy was slowly giving way to increasing doubts about its real objective.

Although at first Duthie thought that the policy of practical training would result in a viable education for Africans, his travels throughout the country gave him the opportunity that no other government official had to see first hand how it was detrimental to the intellectual development of Africans. Believing that he had been used by the colonial establishment to implement a policy he believed was harmful to the educational development of Africans, and that Victorian paternalism was no longer relevant, Duthie decided that it was better to restore his own self image than to be part of implementing a policy he believed was wrong. In 1905 he criticized the policy of practical training: "By the rough and ready plan to make the Natives learn by heart, large numbers of them will have very little opportunity to learn properly. In this way misunderstanding arises between the races."[3] What Duthie was saying, in effect, was that in designing an educational policy to prepare Africans to function as laborers, the government was increasing the prospects of conflict "between the races in the future,"[4] and that if this happened, it would pay a heavier price than would the Africans.

Duthie was suggesting that in seeking to implement the policy of practical training and manual labor, the government was setting the stage for a major racial conflict. The problem was that in 1905, no colonial official was prepared to listen to what appeared to be a cry in the wilderness. However, Duthie had recognized the danger inherent in the belief that the highest role the Africans could fulfill in a colonial society was cheap labor.

In concluding that the colonial government would pay a price for designing and implementing a policy for the education of the Africans different from that for whites, Duthie was opposing the very basis on which that policy was structured and was warning of the consequences. If he had been in Zimbabwe in 1966, the year that the war of independence started, he certainly would have said, "I told you so." It is not surprising that Duthie resigned as inspector of schools in 1901. The influence of his conscience was stronger than the urge to retain his position of power in a system of education that had such great potential for future racial conflict.

Herbert Keigwin Reaffirms the Philosophy of Practical Training

Duthie's resignation posed a major question about the wisdom of the policy of practical training, a situation that suggests a new institutional controversy regarding the ultimate effect of colonial educational policy. For the next fourteen years the educational development of Africans remained in the wilderness unable to take any direction other than meeting the requirements of the Education Ordinance of 1899.

While a heavy cloud of uncertainty hung over the character of African education, the government cooperated fully with white entrepreneurs in taking maximum advantage of the situation. Mining, agriculture, industry, and construction projects continued to expand such centers as Penhalonga, Zwishaware, Mashaba, Hwange, and Kadoma the hub of the economic wheel needed to sustain its political machinery. The policy of practical training was paying large dividends, both political and socioeconomic.

The implications of implementing an educational policy for Africans were quite clear in this situation. The rural African schools, with their emphasis on elementary practical training, produced the cheap labor that the expanding industry needed. The urban schools, with their emphasis on discipline and cleanliness, produced the domestic servants the white home owners needed. The British South Africa Company's educational policy produced Africans who understood little or nothing about the conditions controlling their lives, which is precisely how colonial systems perpetuated themselves. By 1918, the need for cheap labor had reduced the education of Africans to a point where it was so bad that the colonial government tried to do something that would have the appearance of improvement. It therefore named Herbert Keigwin, a leading and influential native commissioner and an uncompromising proponent of the policy of practical training, a one-man commission to study the situation and to submit recommendations for appropriate government action.

But naming Keigwin to undertake this task was the same thing as asking the palace guard to investigate the conduct of the king. It simply could not be done. The question is, what did his purported investigation reveal? In a letter dated December 8, 1919, addressed to his immediate superior, the chief native commissioner, Keigwin attempted to answer those who were criticizing the policy of industrial training and to defend it:

> Considerations have been based on the simple requirements of a backward people. Many could not contemplate that these industries are desirable and profitable, and that they are not an end, but a means to an end. One has to remember that what is wanted among the Natives is something of the old-fashioned craftsmanship of fifty or a hundred years ago.[5]

Although admitting "how lacking I was in technical knowledge"[6] of the situation he was appointed to investigate, Keigwin claimed that he was in a much better position than anyone else to conduct a study of the effect of the policy of practical training on the educational development of Africans. But, as a high-ranking colonial official whose values and attitudes were typically Victorian, Keigwin was unable to predict the possible consequences of an educational policy designed to perpetuate the conditions to which the Africans had been reduced. Further, in appointing Keigwin to conduct a study of this growing problem, the colonial government preferred to risk its own credibility than to take chances with accepting the report of an outsider.

In attempting to justify the policy of industrial training, Keigwin expressed arguments consistent with the larger colonial philosophy regarding the place of Africans in society. In the introduction to his report, Keigwin argued that the policy was intended to improve the mass of the African population rather than a few individuals. In stating, "The policy of raising the mass is infinitely preferred to any scheme for the advancement of a few,"[7] Keigwin concurred with the chief native commissioner for Mashonaland, who had said in 1905, in disagreeing with George Duthie, that Africans who received academic education would not work as laborers.

What is more disturbing about Keigwin's purported study is that it shows neither data nor an explanation of how he secured the information he needed to reach a set of convincing and unbiased conclusions and to substantiate his recommendations. Rather, what one sees is a restatement of the views colonial officials had been expressing since the enactment of the Education Ordinance of 1899. In fact, Keigwin toured South Africa and Britain to solicit the support of influential persons who shared his views on African education. He never carried out any part of his study in Zimbabwe. This is why he sent his report from London.

For these reasons Keigwin rehashed the familiar colonial attitudes toward the educational development of Africans. Among these were the following: that the government did not have sufficient financial resources to support the few talented Africans who could benefit from a good academic education; that it was not in the best interests of the Africans to have a few receive academic education while the rest received practical training and manual labor; and that academic education would not produce laborers but, instead, it would produce political agitators who would exploit the ignorant and uneducated masses to excite racial friction.[8]

What Keigwin really meant, but did not have the courage to say, was that academic education would make it hard to control the rise of self-consciousness among Africans. This is what the colonial government always feared, and it did everything in its power to make it hard, even impossible, for the Africans to acquire it. There is no doubt that Keigwin and his associates wanted the Africans to remain covered by an impenetrable veil of ignorance so that they would be controlled for as long as possible. The denial of a good academic education was universally considered the chief means of sustaining colonialism, for it resulted in the absence of a sharpened mind able to understand the conditions of life of the colonized. To listen to Keigwin argue in favor of sustaining the policy of industrial training and the advantages he claimed accrued from it, is to learn something ironic about the attitude of the colonial officials in general. For example: when Keigwin said: "The industries which would seem to offer the best chance of appealing to the Natives are those to which are most closely allied to those which they are already accustomed. Our objective is to stimulate them to a realization of their own possibilities, thereby contributing to their welfare."[9] This clearly implies that industrial training for Africans was closely related to their fulfilling the labor needs of the country.

With a paternalistic attitude typical of colonial officials and a cynical tongue in cheek, Keigwin went on to add: "The Native has little need for continuous work. He sees nothing amiss with his mode of life. We cannot accept this because we need his cooperation in building up the prospects of the State."[10] This is the same argument Earl Grey had advanced in introducing the first bill on education in 1898. In using the term "cooperation" as a euphemism for training Africans as cheap laborers, Keigwin hoped to persuade those who criticized the colonial government policy to accept the basis of his argument. In stating that the policy of industrial training was intended to eliminate the possibility of competition between Africans and whites, Keigwin pointed out that the curriculum he was recommending for African schools would be similar to the one Booker T. Washington was pursuing at Tuskegee, but added that in Southern Rhodesia, the purpose of industrial education was to ensure economic development of the country and, thus, that of the Africans.

Keigwin attempted to argue what no government official had tried to argue in the past: that the Africans must apply what they learned in school to their daily village activity. In concluding that, "We must make it possible for the educated Native to go back to live among his own people,"[11] Keigwin was trying to make the policy of industrial training appear relevant to the economic needs of rural Africans. But he did not explain how this could be done since Africans who had graduated from those schools were expected to be employed in the service of the whites as laborers.

Keigwin's efforts to justify the policy of industrial training for Africans were most plausible in an aspect he called village industries. He listed seven that he thought should form the core of the curriculum and at the same time would be relevant to the traditional African life-style: tanning hides and skins, simple agriculture, making rope and mats, making baskets, pottery, simple carpentry, and blacksmith work.[12] In urging that the district native commissioners be asked to coordinate and supervise these industries, Keigwin neglected to consider that there was nothing new in them, the Africans, were already experts in all of them. Therefore, there was nothing that could be considered educational in the kind of industries Keigwin was recommending. He was merely adding a colonial flavor to make it palatable to his associates

Domboshawa and Tjolotjo: Making or Sealing the Fate of a Colonial Official?

To give credibility to his proposals, Keigwin recommended that two government industrial schools, one in Mashonaland and the other in Matabeleland, be opened to train African demonstrators, who would assist the native commissioners in making those village industries a success. Domboshawa was opened in 1920, and Tjolotjo in 1921.[13] Keigwin's report impressed his superiors and led to his appointment as director of native development in 1920. Although expressing serious reservations about the plan, the Christian Conference of Southern Rhodesia was generally supportive: "This Conference welcomes the establishment of Native schools by the government."[14]

Keigwin was the man of the hour, or so he thought. Everything he wanted came his way. He was in a position to pull all the strings. His sense of destiny was being realized, and his fate fulfilled. His ideas of education for Africans, or what he claimed to be an education, had elevated him to a new height of popularity among his colleagues in the colonial government. An enthusiastic colonial official who wanted to succeed where he thought Duthie had failed, Keigwin approached his new assignment and responsibility with a firm dedication and a conviction that surprised his superiors. He was prepared to risk his reputation, to put all his eggs in the one basket of an uncertain enterprise. Because he believed that the policy of practical training was a perfect formula for enabling Africans to meet the labor needs of the country and, at the same time, for solving their educational problems, he felt that nothing could go wrong with its implementation. He was to be disappointed.

There is no doubt that Keigwin wanted his plan to serve as a model in all of colonial Africa for many years to come. In arguing at the Christian Conference in 1920 that this was the kind of educational policy the Africans themselves wanted, Keigwin suggested that this would bring them along the road of Western civilization faster than by any other means.[15] No one was prepared to risk a confrontation with a colonial official by showing evidence that would refute much of what he was saying.

Francis Chaplain, who served as British South Africa Company administrator from November 1, 1923, to September 30, 1924, had so much confidence in Keigwin and faith in his plan that he gave him a free hand in doing whatever he thought was right in African education. Thus, Keigwin had become absolute in every way. He was an undisputed authority on African affairs, not only in his self-proclaimed knowledge of the educational programs appropriate to the presumed limited level of intellectual potential of the Africans, but also in that whatever he demanded was done. He had become czar of a new era of colonial thinking and savvy in dealing with the Africans. His receipt of $35,700 to implement his plan shows the extent of his power and influence within the the colonial hierarchy.

Keigwin's ability to attract the interest and the support of influential people in South Africa, Zimbabwe, and Britain was to him a demonstration of the wisdom of a policy he had helped to perfect. Even the skeptical missionaries were so impressed with the plan that they gave it their unqualified support.[16] In the minds of many, Keigwin had formulated a plan of action that would lead to a blueprint for using Africans for what Kenneth Knorr calls "raw materials to be used in the service of the white man."[17] There is no doubt that Keigwin wanted both Domboshawa and Tjolotjo to serve as a centerpiece of his philosophy and as a showcase of his power. He knew that both schools had to succeed because he had staked his reputation and career on the success of the training he wanted them to provide. There was no room for any form of academic activity in their operation. He ordered both schools built to offer practical training and manual labor only.

Throughout the country, and in neighboring countries of southern Africa, excitement had been building about the expected greatness of what everyone called a milestone, a project so rare that anyone who had heard about the plan thought Keigwin was a genius, a colonial superman, finding solutions to chronic educational problems the Africans had faced since formal education began in 1859. He spoke with such authority that he seemed to read the minds of Africans and colonial officials. Indeed, Keigwin, like his mentor, Cecil John Rhodes, had become the E. F. Hutton of the new era in colonial attitudes on the educational development of Africans: When he spoke, everyone listened.

But, just as Rome grew and fell, Keigwin's image of superman began to fall. To his horror and embarrassment, as soon as Domboshawa and Tjolotjo opened their doors, in 1920 and 1921, respectively, the African students demanded more academic education than practical training. The knowledge that the much — heralded plan, the hallmark of preparing Africans to serve the whites might turn out to be a nightmare was frightening and horrifying.

The publicity that had been given the plan, the authority with which he seemed to speak about the educational needs of Africans, and the structure of both schools to eliminate any form of academic education turned Keigwin's brightest hope into an abyss of despair. Slowly but steadily Keigwin was becoming a troubled man, caught between two conflicting positions: the need to sustain a colonial political and socioeconomic status quo and the need to move aggressively away from a policy that appeared to handicap the educational development of Africans. That Domboshawa and Tjolotjo might become white elephants or ghost towns spelled disaster for their author. Suddenly Keigwin, believed to be the genius of colonial political thought process, became a beleaguered man, hopelessly out of touch with reality. In the cruel world of colonial politics, in which a man who was wrong paid the ultimate price, Keigwin groped for rescue where there was none. The ship in which he had placed all his treasure was slowly sinking in the turbulent waters of colonial politics.

His reputation badly tarnished, his political savvy questioned, his authority to speak on behalf of Africans criticized, his administrative skills doubted, and his blueprint a great embarrassment, Keigwin knew that the end of his career was near. The fragile basket into which he had placed his political and philosophical eggs was falling apart. His was the inevitable fate of a colonialist who had gambled everything to elevate his image and leave his name in the records of the colonial government. The thought that he might fail, and that his entire world might collapse before his own eyes, was so devastating that Keigwin was unable to reassess the situation and try something new. Such was the character of colonial politics: The bad and the good often came in one bag. The line between the certain and the speculative was often fragile and thin. One was never sure what would work, the best plans often went astray, and Keigwin was the ultimate victim of his own plan of action.

The question is: What exactly caused Keigwin's demise? When the students at Domboshawa and Tjolotjo threatened to boycott classes if academic education was not provided, Keigwin felt that he had no choice but to resign and remove himself from the controversial situation which he had created. He had served his purpose, but it was now time to go because that purpose did not meet the needs of the Africans.

Both his plan and ideas were things of the past, at least for now. They later found a new champion in George Stark. One must wonder how a man like Keigwin, who seemed to know everything about the needs of the Africans, could make such gross miscalculations as to cause his entire plan to backfire. Was Stark really able to learn anything from the mistakes Keigwin made? These were questions that Stark, like Keigwin, did not consider. In his arrogance, Stark was bound to make the same mistakes as Keigwin.

Harold Jowitt: The Fragile Bridge over Troubled Water

The demands of the African students at Domboshawa and Tjolotjo for an academic education required a complete reevaluation of the educational policy and changes in the plan that had taken Keigwin several years to develop. The problem he faced was that the Africans wanted practical training to be only incidental to good academic education, while he, as a representative of the colonial government, wanted the simple elements of literacy to support practical training. There was no compromise between these positions. For the next four years (1922-1926), the confusion and the disarray that characterized African education as a result of Keigwin's failure spelled the end of his plan. When the Committee on Native Development of 1925 recommended the establishment of the Department of Native Education separate from the Department of Native Affairs,[18] the colonial government found a temporary solution to the embarrassment it had experienced in the failure of Keigwin and his plan. In December 1927, the Department of Native Education was established and $9,520 was allocated for its implementation.[19] Harold Jowitt, a far more intellectual person than Keigwin,[20] and who had 14 years of experience in education for Africans in South Africa, was appointed its first director. He was assisted by four inspectors.[21]

Jowitt seemed equal to the task of rebuilding the shattered image of the colonial plan that had failed under Keigwin. He was an educator of imposing stature, a dynamic leader of immense popularity, an administrative technocrat, and an innovator willing to risk his reputation in order to try new ideas. His enthusiasm for success was a reasonable substitute for a lack of experience with the political conditions that governed how things were done in Zimbabwe.

A relentless negotiator and a cunning diplomat, Jowitt had an approach to his new responsibilities that was a breath of fresh air for the missionaries, who felt that under Keigwin their influence was slipping. Jowitt seemed to have healthy relations with the various segments of the communities involved in African education. In his desire to succeed where he thought Duthie and Keigwin had failed, Jowitt had become a fragile bridge over troubled water. With respect to the education of Africans, he tried to mediate in the conflict between political philosophy and the reality of human existence, between past policies and a new idealism. He tried to balance between politically expedient programs and what was real, between the African desire for a good academic education as a means of eliminating the old colonial stereotypes and the shackles that bound their minds, and the colonial intent to have them provide cheap labor. He tried to satisfy both the Africans' desire for a good education and the expressed wish of the white entrepreneurs to sustain their economic and political power base through cheap labor, which only the Africans could provide. The conditions of the times made Jowitt's task much harder than that of any of his predecessors. He knew that his options were few, and that he had to play his limited number of cards carefully. There was no room for error, and the stakes were high. Believing that it was possible to strike a working balance between these conflicting positions, Jowitt began his task with a clear understanding of the importance of his mission. In his first annual report submitted in 1928, Jowitt acknowledged that he faced some rather serious and unexpected problems, and went on to discuss some of them:

> The non-existence of data and records regarding the work, the thinking that education for Natives is a step-child receiving the crumbs from the dinner table of the accredited educational family, the absence of any qualified officials in Native education, all tend to preclude the development of an adequate system of official records and constitute the fundamental problems in Native education.[22]

It is quite clear that Jowitt was expressing disappointment over the disorganized and haphazard manner in which Keigwin had carried out his responsibility. In saying so, he was suggesting how difficult his own task would be. That there were "practically no data bearing upon definite conditions in over 90% of the schools, upon the teaching staffs and their qualifications or duties, upon the number of boys and girls, upon the rate of increase in the number of schools"[23] suggests the extent of Keigwin's obsession with the policy of practical training at the expense of every other aspect of the educational process. Jowitt was disappointed to discover that Keigwin, whom everyone credited with solving problems of African education, did not keep accurate records of the work he did in such a critical area of national policy.

Criticizing Keigwin's plan as an attempt to institutionalize African life in a mechanical fashion,[24] and his policy of village industries as "lacking clarity and definition, and so failed to reach a central unifying principle to serve in the development of criteria,"[25] Jowitt warned of the consequences of continuing the traditional colonial attitude that "the security of one race can be ensured by the repression of another."[26] He did not hesitate to express his opinion that Keigwin's plan was nothing less than a repression of Africans, both mentally and politically. There is no doubt that Jowitt disagreed fundamentally with Keigwin's policy and plan. His argument that "The Africans must not be trained by an inferior kind of education to function as better hewers of wood and drawers of water for their white masters"[27] was intended to refute what a high-ranking colonial official had promoted during the debate on the Education Ordinance bill of 1912, a position Keigwin had supported.[28]

Jowitt then established his own set of aims for African education. These included "breaking down the separate compartments which have been created by different government departments,"[29] creating affinities between the educational process and efforts to restore the position of detribalized Africans, creating a working balance between academic education and practical education, seeking full cooperation between the missionaries and the government in determining educational objectives and priorities, returning the benefits of African labor to improve the school system, training teachers in sufficient numbers and at a sufficient level so that the educational process would be improved, and designing the curriculum so that students would be adequately prepared to relate what they learned to seeking solutions to problems of political and socioeconomic injustice.[30]

This was an impressive list of things to be done and objectives to be fulfilled. Would his superiors allow him to accomplish them all? Jowitt was certainly trying to do things that no previous official had tried in African education. But if there was a major problem that would handicap him, it was the traditional colonial policy, for allowing Jowitt to fulfill these objectives would represent a radical change of the structure of society. The colonial government could not allow that to happen and still hope that the whites would continue to exert their traditional claim of exclusive political and socioeconomic superiority.

How can one see Jowitt's efforts to improve African education? One might have the impression that he was a white liberal, a Don Quixote charging the giant windmills of traditionally colonial negative attitudes toward the educational development of Africans. The truth of the matter is that this was the only option open to him. How could he bring about a much -needed change in a beleaguered system without changing its fundamental structure? How could he formulate a policy intended to bring about a rapid advancement of Africans without initiating change in the thought processes of the colonial officials?

There is no doubt that Jowitt knew that the change the Africans would accept was the introduction of a good academic education, that they had no objection to practical training as such but recognized that by itself, it was limited in what it offered them for the future.[31] He also knew that the change his superiors would accept was the strengthening of the policy of practical training. How was he going to reconcile these extremely conflicting positions? He needed the wisdom of Solomon to play the game of colonial political hide-and-seek between the white entrepreneurs and the Africans in order to maintain his perspective.

In his annual report for 1930, Jowitt attempted to furnish some answers to the question of how he was going to present his juggling act in the arena of increasing conflicts:

> It seems fairly evident that progress was made during the year. It may not be so clearly realized that this would not have been possible without taking other factors into consideration. Such factors include missionaries, who continue to spend themselves unreservedly in the cause of Native development.
>
> The critics of our work claim that we differ from them in that they alone regard things as they really are. It is our conviction that the best products of this work will gradually add to the dynamic strength of this country.[32]

Jowitt was able to speak with this high degree of confidence because he had gained the support of the missionaries. Unlike the rigid Keigwin, he was open to new ideas and was sensitive to the educational needs of Africans, which the missionaries claimed to represent. His ability to perceive what was possible in light of what was ideal gave him the balance he needed as he walked this delicate political tightrope. But his inability to convince his superiors that both practical training and academic education had an important place in the education of Africans was the gusty wind that threw him off balance and brought his act to an untimely end only seven years after it had started.

That Jowitt, unlike Keigwin, was sensitive to the views of the missionaries about the importance of religious education gave him an advantage over his associates within the colonial government. Therefore, from the very beginning of his tenure, Jowitt enjoyed the trust and confidence of the missionaries, a group whose support he needed to carry out the task of bringing about a much-needed reform in African education. That the missionaries did not have the same trust and confidence in Stark caused him some serious problems.[33] Within five years of his appointment as director of native education, Jowitt had an impressive list of recognized accomplishments. At the same time he felt restrained and handicapped by the negative attitudes and actions of his superiors. This was so disturbing that he described 1932 as "a year of arrested development, a colorless record"[34] of failure to accomplish what had to be done. Among the actions Jowitt discussed as contributing to this "arrested development" was the issuance of Government Notice Number 676 of 1929 and Government Notice Number 144 of 1932, each reducing by 15 percent the funds he needed to carry out his work — without advising him of the fact.

One can conclude that the government took this action to register its disapproval of Jowitt's "liberal" views on the education of Africans, especially his belief in the importance of good academic education, and what it perceived as his acquiescence to missionary demands for a forceful approach to the problems the educational process was experiencing. One can also see that early in his tenure, Jowitt did not enjoy the absolute support of his superiors in the way that Keigwin did. Translated into practical realities this situation put Jowitt in a precarious position.

Two questions must now be asked: How long would Jowitt's superiors allow him to continue the course of innovation he had charted in 1927? What, exactly, were the problems that handicapped his work? One finds an answer to the second question in what Jowitt said in his last annual report, in 1933. In recognizing that until he was appointed the director of the department, Native Education, the African of Zimbabwe "moved in an orbit of his own, but factors of significance have altered this for all time,"[35] Jowitt seemed to suggest that the traditional attitude among colonial officials was the major problem that limited his ability to fulfill his responsibility.

Not only did Jowitt's superiors disapprove of his innovative ideas, they also thought he was moving too fast to dismantle a policy that dated from the enactment of the Education Ordinance in 1899. The truth of the matter was that Jowitt disagreed with his superiors over the fundamental purpose of education for Africans. There is no question that while the core of the colonial government officials believed the essential structure of African education must remain one of practical training, Jowitt felt that this form of education was totally inadequate to meet the needs of the students and to prepare them for the future because it was designed to train Africans "to function as hewers of wood and drawers of water for their white masters."

This was a conflict situation for which there was no ready solution. Jowitt's superiors could not consider adjusting an old practice, and Jowitt refused to compromise principle for political expediency. This situation spelled a parting of ways between Jowitt and the colonial hierarchy. He had given his best, but it was not good enough. His brand of liberalism and his superiors' brand of conservatism had shattered the delicate bridge over the troubled water, creating a situation in which a rapidly rising flood of charged emotions swept away everything in its path.

In 1933, the relationship between Jowitt and his superiors had deteriorated to the point where it was impossible to restore. To the chief native commissioner, Jowitt's immediate superior, and the one most vocal against his innovative approach to African education, Jowitt directed a stinging attack. He could no longer listen to the commissioner's urging him not to change a system that they both knew was doing no one any good. Jowitt went on to say:

> The problem of education is the problem of a community making the most of it. The problem of the school or of a school system, is merely a chapter in that more inclusive problem. School is important, but the school unrelated and unacquainted with the world in which the students live, is an impertinence.[36]

Concluding that the policy of practical training for Africans was "in the long run, an immoral institution,"[37] Jowitt was viewing the problem from its proper educational and intellectual perspective. He argued therefore that because education must be universal, there was no reason to practice racial discrimination. He called the latter an immoral act coming from an immoral institution. Unfortunately, Jowitt's superiors were unwilling and unable to see things from this perspective. Rather, they saw them from the perspective of political expediency. Thus, there was no common ground between Jowitt and his superiors. This fundamental difference of philosophy and opinion was the major problem that handicapped his ability to discharge his responsibility well.

The answer to the question of how long his superiors would allow Jowitt to continue the course he had charted is found in his resignation, in total disgust, in November 1934, nearly seven years after he was appointed. It is surprising that Jowitt, considering the liberal views he held, was able to stay in office that long. Franklin Parker, who interviewed Jowitt at his home in Uganda in 1960, told the author in 1988, "Jowitt had a vision of Africa of the future. He could not fit in the system of which he was a part."[38]

Summary and Conclusion

The immediate impact of Jowitt's resignation was that its exposure of the farce of the policy of practical training, not that anyone believed in its claimed viability as a form of education designed to promote the development of Africans, but in what benefit the colonial government obtained from it, both economically and politically. It revealed the two sides to the question of African education. On the one hand was the obsession of the colonial government with cheap labor, which only the Africans who had undergone practical training could provide. On the other hand, George Duthie and Harold Jowitt saw the educational process as going far beyond the purpose of education itself. To both men it had become the question of imposing Victorian beliefs on race and politics. Because the colonial government was not willing to see the error of its policy, the educational process for Africans lost the purpose for which it had been instituted. The colonial government officials saw the educational process as merely a channel to the ultimate goal: perpetual white political and socioeconomic power.

As one looks back, beginning with the enactment of the Education Ordinance of 1899, one is at a loss to understand why the colonial government was unwilling to consider alternative approaches to the policy it defined and pursued. George Duthie and Harold Jowitt were not the only white people to recognize the weakness inherent in that policy. Even more tragic is that after Jowitt resigned, the colonial government found ways not of ending an inadequate policy but of strengthening it. This is how George Stark entered the picture. The rest of this volume will address his philosophy of African education, his policy and how he implemented it, and the effect it had on African education and institutional relations in Zimbabwe from 1934 to 1954.

Notes

1. George Duthie, Inspection Report of St. Augustine's School, November 1901. In St. Augustine's School Records.
2. The Methodist Church, Official Journal of the Methodist Church, (1901), p. 5.
3. George Duthie, "Education in Rhodesia" in British South Africa Association for the Advancement of Science, Vol. 4, (1905), pp. 321-324.
4. Ibid. p. 322
5. Herbert Keigwin, letter dated December 8, 1919, addressed to the chief native commissioner. In Zimbabwe National Archives.
6. Ibid.
7. Southern Rhodesia, The Report of the Commission of Inquiry into Industrial Development of Natives (Herbert Keigwin,chairman). Ref. A7/457.1920, p. 3.
8. Ibid. p. 4
9. Ibid. p. 6
10. Ibid. p. 8
11. Ibid. p. 9
12. Ibid. p. 10
13. See Chapter 4 of this volume for enrollment figures at both schools from 1933 to 1953.
14. Southern Rhodesia Christian Conference, Statement responding to the opening of Domboshawa and Tjolotjo, July 8, 1921. In Zimbabwe National Archives.
15. Ibid.
16. The Southern Rhodesia Christian Conference, 1920.
17. Kenneth Knorr, British Colonial Theories (Toronto: University of Toronto Press, 1974), p. 377.
18. Southern Rhodesia, Committee on Native Development, 1925, p. 58.
19. Southern Rhodesia: Legislative Debates, 1927. In the same year he was appointed director of native education (1927), Jowitt wrote a masters thesis at the University of Cape Town, "The Reconstruction of African Education in Southern Rhodesia." It attempted to argue against a set of Victorian views and attitudes were still influencing the policy of the colonial officials on the educational development of the Africans.
20. Southern Rhodesia, The Report of on the Committee on Education, 1943.
21. They were J. H. Farquhur, Salisbury Circuit; W.H. Seaton, Mutare Circuit; A. R. Mather, Victoria (Masvingo) Circuit; and H. C. Finkle, Bulawayo Circuit; Finkle succeeded Stark in 1954.
22. Harold Jowitt, The Annual Report of the Director of Native Education, 1928, p. 1.
23. Ibid. p. 6.
24. Ibid. p. 7.
25. Ibid. p. 6.
26. Ibid. p. 41.
27. Ibid. p. 7. See also Chapter 1 of this volume for the letter written by a government official to The Rhodesia Herald, June 28, 1912, suggesting that the Africans must be trained to function as "hewers of wood and drawers of water for their white masters." It seems, therefore, that Jowitt knew his history well.
28. Ibid. p. 9.
29. Ibid. p. 8.
30. Ibid. p. 10.
31. Beginning in 1952, the graduates of Domboshawa, Tjolotjo, and other industrial schools, such as Tegwani and Mt. Selinda, were left in a social and economic limbo when efforts were being directed toward academic education.
32. Harold Jowitt, The Annual Report of the Director of Native Education, 1930, p. 47.
33. See Chapter 3 of this volume for details.
34. Harold Jowitt, The Annual Report of the Director of Native Education, 1932, p. 1. One cannot minimize the effect of this historical precedent on similar situation facing African education in 1964. Charles S. Davies, then secretary for African education, characterized African education in that year as "the year of troubles," caused primarily by the massive boycott of schools because they were inadequately preparing Africans for an effective role in society.
35. Harold Jowitt, The Annual Report of the Director of Native Education, 1933, p. 22.
36. Ibid. p. 23.
37. Ibid. p. 25.
38. Franklin Parker, during a conversation with the author in Flagstaff, Arizona, August 31, 1988. In 1960 Parker published *Education and African Development in Southern Rhodesia* (Columbus, Ohio: Kappa Delta Pi), which discussed Jowitt's and Stark's policies.

3
Stark's Philosophy of Education for Africans: Relating the School to Tribal Life and Colonial Conditions

The fundamental objective in African education must be to make an effort to bind more closely the ties between the school and tribal life. — George Stark, 1930

The Effect of Jowitt's Resignation

Jowitt's resignation in November 1934 raised far more serious doubts about his successor than about the course he had charted for the development of African education. George Stark, the successor, put the resignation into perspective when he wrote, "The very important part which he contributed to Native development during his term of office will be realized with the passage of the years. His going has been a great loss."[1] Whether Stark was sincere must be regarded as an important factor to be considered in light of the major developments in which he played a major role.

Stark's recognition that Jowitt's resignation was a cause of great anxiety among missionaries shows the extent of the apprehension among the missionaries concerning Stark as Jowitt's successor. Trying to remove himself as the cause of their displeasure, Stark appears to place the reasons for their concern elsewhere:

> There is tenseness due to an uncertainty which they have felt regarding the future of Native education. This uneasiness found expression at the Christian Conference in June and December. The resignation of the Director was a contributory cause of this uneasiness.[2]

What Stark did not say is that the missionaries had learned to trust Jowitt because he was sensitive to the needs of their schools. That the chief native commissioner, Jowitt's immediate superior, openly criticized him in 1933 for moving too fast and outside the official policy[3] did not make Stark's task any easier because there was a strong feeling that Jowitt was forced out of office by Stark. Therefore, the significance of Jowitt's resignation is that it created a new chasm between colonial officials and church leaders, mainly because he was succeeded by Stark,[4] a man whose ideas were very similar to those of Herbert Keigwin.

George Stark: The Man and His Mission

It is quite evident that Stark became a controversial figure as soon as he assumed office because his philosophy of education for Africans was radically different from that of Jowitt. The obvious question arises: Who was George Stark? Part of the answer comes from Jowitt himself, who portrays him as dedicated zealot, a team player who was willing to take risks to ensure that any cause he was fighting for succeeded. This is why Jowitt said of him:

> Mr. Stark places on record the various ways in which our endeavors must be tackled effectively. He believes that the road is long, progress along it is slow. But only by keeping sight of the ultimate goal can we avoid being disheartened.[5]

This statement reveals that Stark was an ardent colonialist who slowly paved his way to the top by convincing his superiors that they could count on him to pull his full weight in the forthcoming test of wills regarding the conduct of African education. The circumstances that brought Stark to join Jowitt's staff in 1929 from Lovedale, a leading Church of Scotland school for Africans in South Africa, are as interesting as they are intriguing. It is clear that Jowitt knew him while both men were in Natal, but it is not clear whether they knew each other well as colleagues. How could Jowitt bring in a man whose views of the Africans were radically different from his own, a man who appeared to begin working against him as soon as he joined his staff?

Stark did not show his ultra conservative views until he was in office although there were signals. Yet, despite their wide differences of opinion and views on the important issues that would determine their success or failure, Jowitt was apparently impressed with Stark as a loyal and a hardworking associate. At Lovedale, Stark had proved his loyalty to his superiors and his dedication to the objectives he was called upon to fulfill. He had no time for recreation or humor; he was always serious.[6]

Stark attempted to make up for his lack of intellectual depth with a total devotion to the educational policy the colonial government had formulated, just as he had done at Lovedale. He was not an innovator, nor was he particularly alert to trends and critical issues of the day. His limited experience with Africans at Lovedale would hurt, rather than help him, in assuming and carrying out his new responsibility. His insensitivity to the real educational needs of the Africans demonstrated an almost callous attitude typical of most colonial officials. Stark assumed office one year after Godfrey Huggins was elected prime minister in 1933. The two men entered into a 20-year partnership that was destined to leave a black mark on the pages of the history of education for Africans in colonial Zimbabwe.

As soon as Stark joined the Department of Native Education, he learned to function under the influence of political factors that forced him to choose loyalty to Jowitt as his superior or loyalty to the colonial government as an institution. That he chose the latter was really not surprising. To show that he was a political game player and to demonstrate his devotion to Huggins Stark persuaded him to allay the fears that the missionaries had expressed over Jowitt's resignation. He did this not because he believed this was the right thing to do, but because he wanted to gain the ground he needed to design his own set of policies. Huggins, in order to improve his own image, agreed to do that.

That Stark was the one to put this matter into perspective shows how new political alliances were beginning to form during the first few months after Jowitt resigned:

> The prime minister considered it expedient to reassure the missionary representatives at the meetings of the Advisory Board for Native Department that it was not the intention of the government to discontinue the policy adopted in previous years for Native education, but merely to bring about a change in the method of administration.[7]

It turned out that there was a great deal more than a change in administrative style from Jowitt to Stark. On the advice of the chief native commissioner, the high-ranking colonial official who had severely criticized Jowitt, Huggins appointed Stark acting director of native development for one year. In doing so, the designation "Native Education Department" was temporarily discontinued. Upon Stark's confirmation as permanent director that designation was reactivated. For the next twenty years Stark, in close cooperation with Huggins and consistent with larger colonial objectives, formulated and implemented his own policy. One cannot resist reaching the conclusion that the missionaries had reached: that Jowitt was double-crossed by an ambitious zealot, a subordinate who had a set of motives and objectives of his own.

To understand Stark's mission, one must understand and appreciate Jowitt's accomplishments. In many respects Jowitt's tenure was epoch-making. It had been a time of expansion in important areas of African education. The quality of the village teacher, the backbone of the entire educational system, had improved greatly. The proportion of untrained teachers had dropped from 76 percent to 39 percent between 1928 and 1933.[8] By stressing the relationship between the educational process and finding solutions to human problems, Jowitt had become a pioneer in making education relevant to the human condition in a colonial setting. Stark had an entirely different idea of relating the school to the human condition: confine Africans to tribal life and train them to function as cheap laborers.

In 1931 alone a record number of new schools came into existence for the major purpose of training Africans to relate the educational process to collective action in seeking solutions to national and human problems. Jowitt believed that once this relationship was established, Africans could be educated to hold more important positions in society. For him, the schools were there to serve genuine human needs. For Stark they were there to confine Africans to tribal settings.

There were other important differences in philosophy of education for Africans between Jowitt and Stark. For Jowitt, the schools were there to train the Africans to assume responsibility in a larger social context, and he rejected the thinking that Tawse Jollie, Hugh Williams, and other colonialists expressed: that they must be trained to serve the interests of whites. This is why in 1930 Jowitt authorized the opening of the following schools for the academic year 1931, compared with the number of schools in 1927, when he assumed office:

Denomination	Number of Schools		Denomination	Number of Schools	
	1927	1931		1927	1931
Church of England	9	11	African Methodist	2	4
Wesleyan Methodist	4	7	Roman Catholic	1	2
American Board	3	5	Church of Sweden	1	2
Salvation Army	2	3	American Methodist	1	2
Total	18	26		5	10

Source: Harold Jowitt, Annual Report, 1930, p. 11.

In addition to these accomplishments, Jowitt had gained the confidence of both the missionaries and the Africans as a man who was genuinely interested not only in their educational development but also in finding solutions to the problems they faced.

Jowitt's accomplishments made him very difficult to succeed, and Stark's mission a very difficult task indeed. But an enormous ego and a burning personal ambition to succeed at a level that had not been seen in many years combined with the support he received from Huggins and the chief native commissioner to give him a considerable advantage. From the beginning of his 20-year tenure, Stark went out of his way to prove that he was the man for the job. In a real sense, he and Huggins knew that their destinies were intertwined, the success or failure of the one determining the success or failure of the other.

Therefore, to understand Stark's philosophy of education for Africans, his character, and his mission is also to understand Huggins's political ideology and programs. That is why Stark moved forcefully to establish an agenda that not only reversed Jowitt's programs but also strengthened the essential elements of Keigwin's plan of reducing the education of Africans to basic village industries in tribal settings that would ensure a steady supply of cheap labor. The colonial entrepreneurs during Stark's tenure knew that he shared Huggins's desire to remove African education from a course of development that would have serious political implications for the colonial government. In Chapters 5 and 6 we discuss how this thinking aided the formation of the alliance between Huggins and Stark and how, in turn, it shaped the character of African education.

Stark's aim of reducing the educational process for Africans to a tribal setting did not permit the formulation of an educational policy that would elevate them to a level where they would understand the context or the character of a society of which they were part. This is why he advanced his basic philosophy, saying in 1930, "The fundamental objective in African education must be to make an effort to bind more closely the ties between the school and tribal life."[9] It meant reducing education for Africans to a tribal level that did not allow them to participate in national affairs, except to function as cheap laborers. This, in essence, was the major thrust of Stark's mission.

Conditions of African Life and Education under Stark

The progress that Jowitt had made in improving the village school profoundly affected African education. He had faced difficulties that no previous colonial official was willing to face. The greatest of these difficulties was to make education for Africans relevant to their developmental needs. Although he did not quite succeed in that endeavor, he managed to lay a foundation on which he hoped his successor would build a new and dynamic program for the development of Africans. But under Stark things took an entirely different course. As soon as Stark took office, the education of the Africans began to deteriorate rapidly. Under Jowitt the ratio of teachers to students was 1:40. Under Stark it was 1:45. Jowitt had proposed that the annual aid grants to schools be $45.00 per school per student based on average daily attendance, as originally provided in the Education Ordinance of 1899 (as amended from time to time). Under Stark the grant was reduced to $40.00 by 1935 because he did not feel that such an amount should be allocated for the kind of education offered to Africans.[10]

Shortly before he left office, Jowitt had proposed that all African schools receive annual aid grants to assist in the development of a dynamic educational system over a period of time. In 1935, however, Stark formulated and recommended a new policy that his superiors readily accepted:

> The African schools would have to depend upon other sources of support. This may be done through moneys sent to the missions from overseas. But with depleted revenue from overseas, the missions have to strive more and more to arrive at a basis of self-support. They have to depend upon the native people themselves to give added financial assistance.[11]

Remembering that in the same year, 1935, free and compulsory education was introduced for white students, the new policy imposed severe difficulties on African students, as Stark knew. This was exactly what he wanted, because it was consistent with broader objectives of the colonial government.

Before he left office, Jowitt had recommended that the starting salary for a certificated male teacher be $70.00 per year. He suggested that since the country was recovering from the Great Depression, this proposal would provide Africans with encouragement to rebuild their shattered economic base and provide an incentive in their struggle to secure meaningful education in the future. Stark not only recommended rejection of the plan but also held the annual salary of those teachers to $66.00. Was Stark sincere when he suggested that Jowitt's resignation was a great loss? Clearly he appears to have ignored an important factor: that because the policy of practical training had reduced Africans to conditions of bare subsistence it was virtually impossible to expect them to make a substantial financial contribution to the education of their children.

It is evident that Stark's solution to this problem meant a further reduction in the educational opportunity for Africans. In concluding that "In order that budgets may be balanced, the salaries of teachers have to be cut and many may have to be turned away,"[12] Stark proved to be a true colonial bureaucrat whose solutions to the problems of African education were often based on what he considered to be in the best interests of the whites and of the colonial government . African education suffered a severe setback under Stark, which suggests that the motivation which appears to be central to his policies is how African education could best serve the interests of the colonial status quo, rather than how it could best promote the advancement of Africans. Within the conditions that influenced this thinking, the attitudes, and the formulation of policies, Stark's views stand out in sharp contrast with those of Jowitt. He enjoyed the total confidence and full support of his superiors for 20 years, but during that time the adverse effect of his policies on the educational advancement of Africans had negative implications that hurt both Huggins and Stark himself. Let us discuss how this happened.

Stark's Philosophy of Education for Africans: Its Three Inseparable Elements

A question now arises: Why did Stark pursue a policy that in effect meant a reversal of the progressive policy Jowitt had pursued? The answer lies in Stark's philosophy of education for Africans. There is no question that he rejected Jowitt's apparent liberalism toward Africans and felt that the traditional colonial attitude toward their education must be viewed only from the perspective of its importance for their ability to function as cheap laborers and to live in tribal settings.

Three essential elements formed Stark's philosophy of education for Africans, all of them consistent with the traditional colonial attitude. The first was that education must be of simple and practical, and must not include academic material beyond basic literacy. The second was that African education must be confined to helping the African population to relate to tribal life or, as he suggested after an inspection visit to Masasa School on 1930, "to bind ties between the school and tribal life."

What Stark failed to see was that rural and tribal life, as it existed before the establishment of the colonial government was quite complete and sufficient to meet the needs of the people. However, once there had been an intrusion into that cultural setting, such as that resulting from colonization, it was no longer possible to retain its characteristic components. Stark's inability to develop a viable alternative diminished the thrust of his mission. It was therefore meaningless for Stark to demand that the educational process, which was not African in its origin and content, be related to the African tribal setting. Nevertheless, that was how Stark saw it, and that was what he set out to accomplish as a viable educational objective. In failing to see the problems that implementing his philosophy was creating for Africans, Stark inadvertently helped to create conditions for a major conflict in the future.

The third element of Stark's philosophy of education for Africans was the introduction of basic reading and writing, to enable the students to carry on the process of practical training. The disturbing feature of this element is that Stark wanted to separate its intended limited value to both tribal settings and practical training from its effect on the rise of African consciousness. But with the inauguration of the first African National Congress in 1933, he discovered that this could not be done without a reaction from the Africans. Stark and Huggins were then faced with a larger problem of literacy: How much of it could they introduce without indirectly aiding broader implications?

Unwilling to risk the rise of African consciousness through basic literacy, and unwilling to forgo the importance of practical training that basic literacy made possible, the two allies faced a dilemma. As the lesser of two evils, they considered the possibility of forcing practical training without basic literacy. But an outcry from the missionaries exposed the plan, and they were forced to abandon it. However, Stark considered these three elements to be inseparable, neatly linked to give coherence to the pursuit of a policy designed to benefit the white entrepreneurs.

As soon as his appointment as director of native education was confirmed in 1935, Stark moved aggressively to formulate his own ideas consistent with his philosophy of education for Africans. In stating, "If the foundations of Native education are to be well laid, there must be an emphasis placed upon the village school system,"[13] Stark was advancing his argument that by the very nature of its intended objective, African education must be closely related to tribal life. This was essentially why he rejected the view that education was universal, and cannot be designed with the tribal or racial background of its recipients in mind.

In arguing that the education of Africans "must not be a preparation for life in the urban areas,"[14] Stark was attempting to put distance between the universal definition of education and his own definition of African education. It did not matter to him that he was being contradictory in taking this position. His inability to resolve the dilemma that he faced compounded his problems. There is no question that in saying, "By attendance at boarding schools, Native pupils get a detest for tribal life. The objective in Native education should be to place more emphasis on tribal bias,"[15] Stark was making a distinction between the educational objectives for Africans and those for whites. He did not envisage a time when education would help build bridges of racial understanding as the best security for whites. As far as he was concerned, the two races must remain apart forever, and education must help in that process. This is a classic example of colonial contradiction that created elements of a major racial conflict in the future.

Stark supported the major recommendation of the Carter Commission of 1925:

> However desirable it may be that members of the two races should live together side by side, we are convinced that in practice, for generations to come, such a policy is not practical or in the best interests of the two races until the Natives have advanced very much further on the path of civilization.[16]

By doing this he was, in essence, strengthening an old colonial belief. For this reason he stressed in 1935 his belief that Africans must never have contact with an urban white environment because it would have an artificial influence on their tribal life.

To emphasize the importance of practical training as viable education for the Africans, Stark advanced a philosophy that had a special appeal to colonial officials: "True education does not come from books, but passes from person to person. The efficacy of the teacher depends on what he is, rather than on what he knows. This is why this department emphasizes the character training of the Native children in this colony."[17] He neglected to consider the reality of the fact that a teacher is a product of education, and, therefore, what the teacher teaches is a product of what he or she knows, an outcome of what he or she has learned.

However, if Stark believed in this philosophy, why did the colonial government introduce free and compulsory education for white students in 1935? Why did it enact the Education Ordinance of 1899, with heavy emphasis on rigorous academic education for white students? Was he suggesting that because white education was heavily academic, white students were therefore miseducated, or was he using this viewpoint to justify his own philosophy of practical training for Africans? There is little doubt that the latter was the case.

In seeking ways to make his philosophy applicable to the education of Africans, during the next three years, Stark formulated an aspect of his philosophy that entailed modification of the mastery of basic literacy to place more emphasis on character training as an added dimension of practical training . He did this so that the Africans who came to work in the growing industries in urban areas would retain their distinctive rural background and, as he argued in 1930, the ties between the school and tribal life would be strengthened. Hence, in 1936 he personally drafted the revision of Government Notice Number 676 of 1929 to ensure that aid grants reflected that reality.[18]

Here there is something even more disturbing than what meets the eye. The nature of human relationships in the colonial setting implied an assumed inferiority of the Africans. By psychologically conditioning them to believe that they were strangers or visitors in urban areas, the colonial officials succeeded in alienating them from more meaningful roles in society. For example, all Africans who came to work in urban areas were discouraged from bringing their families along. They lived in small housing units owned by the city government, and could not buy their own homes.These are still among the tactics that the South African government uses to control Africans.

An interesting aspect of Stark's philosophy becomes clear in the developments that began to unfold in 1936. Because of the increasing control that Stark, as a representative of the colonial government, was exercising over the conduct of African education, public opinion seemed to indicate that the government might as well assume responsibility for running the African schools. He took this opportunity to restate his philosophy in a more powerful way. Wishing to make a distinction between the views of the chief native commissioner and his own, Stark argued:

> Even among missionaries are those who would welcome the taking over by the government of the educational system for Natives. This attitude appears to be based on the assumption that there is clear-cut division between education and religion. Education, by secular definition, is regarded as the concern of the state. It is suggested, however, that it may not be in the best interests of Native education to divorce religion from life because the school is one agent that leads pupils to a fuller life.[19]

What few people knew at the time was that this was clearly a strategy to increase Stark's power to control the character of African education, because he wanted the public to believe that the missionaries still played a role in it. Stark was even more forceful in advancing his philosophy of education for the Africans when he cautioned against a relaxed approach to it:

> Being so powerful as it is, education is a dangerous instrument in the hands of those, who because of their anti-social tendencies, use it for purposes contrary to the welfare of any group of people whose traditions differ fundamentally from those of European race which determines the course of civilization. For Natives, the school requires constant, painstaking and systematic directive supervision.[20]

There is no doubt that Stark wanted the missionaries to act as agents of the government in implementing his policy by making it look like they were equal partners in an endeavor that they considered important. But, to Stark, what was important was that his own philosophy of African education was prevailing.

In 1937, seeing an opportunity to enhance his status among missionaries, Stark successfully persuaded the Christian Conference to pass a resolution at its annual meeting:

> That after 1942 no European will be approved as a teacher unless such a person holds a teachers certificate approved by the Department. That if possible before 1942 superintendents of village schools without teaching qualifications should be given an opportunity to attend a training course.[21]

This resolution was quite consistent with Stark's philosophy of having the education of Africans relate to tribal life. But this was only a prelude to his altering the plan that Jowitt had introduced in 1929, that of training Africans under the Jeanes program,[22] to supervise village schools in accordance with his philosophy of the relationship between the school and tribal life.

Admitting in 1938 that his philosophy of African education had become a subject of "conflicting ideologies and controversial debate,"[23] Stark felt compelled to defend and justify it:

> The underlying principles which govern the course of Native education, reading and writing, do not matter until the material basis of living has been assured. In no profession is the fortune of the individual's work, however humble his lot, more dependent upon his own skills and adjustment.[24]

There is no doubt that Stark was defending his controversial philosophical position that for Africans, good education did not come from books — meaning, of course, that academic education was bad for them because it did not relate to tribal life. Another aspect of Stark's philosophy that he refused to give up was his belief that the African teacher must be trained to teach his students to live under tribal conditions. He therefore went on to argue:

> The most enlightened propaganda must fail if it is disseminated among primitive people still in the grip of superstition, ignorance, and age-old custom. Character is the most important to the development of the African in his emergence from barbarism. Education for Natives must equip them to deal with their environment and fit them to live in their own conditions of life.[25]

For Stark, relating the Africans to their tribal environment and conditions could best be done by training local Africans, whom he considered better able to understand their importance to traditional African life than a white teacher trained in an overseas institution.

There is a definite relationship between this argument and what Stark tried to promote in 1943. Claiming that the war had taken a heavy toll on finances and personnel, he painted a dark picture of African education in the immediate future:

> The shortage of European teachers for native schools grows ever more serious. There is a rapid deterioration in the quality of the school work. The school system is being adversely affected through the wartime difficulties. This presents a problem which is not likely to be satisfactorily solved until after the war is over.[26]

Stark seems to argue that it was just as well that white teachers were not available in sufficient numbers to meet the need, and that in future it might be well to train Africans as teachers of their own people. One does not have to look far to see that what Stark really feared was that the white teachers, because they came from a cultural and social environment different from that of the African teachers, would give their African students something more than his policy allowed: the elements of self-consciousness. In allowing white teachers to teach African students, the tribal environment to which he wanted them to be restricted would begin to fall away. This, in essence, was the reason for wanting to train African teachers.

This was also why Stark vigorously argued that a sufficient number of locally trained teachers must be produced in order to make sense out of his policy of relating education to tribal settings. A factor closely related to this argument was that the African teachers were paid only a fraction of what the white teachers were paid. The reality of this situation forced Stark to contradict himself in what he had argued in 1938: that in order to have an effective practical training program for Africans, only white teachers should be hired, since the African teachers could not be trusted to undertake such a major responsibility[27] because it entailed the implementation of a policy they did not understand. If Stark's contradictory positions were intended to keep the critics of his philosophy off-guard, the strategy did not work because the missionaries became increasingly suspicious about why he was formulating the policy that he did.

By 1943, Stark's philosophy of African education came into conflict with that of the Education Committee, which took issue with his definition of the purpose of education. In stating its own philosophy, the committee argued:

> Schools of every type fulfill their proper purpose in so far as they foster the free growth of individuality, helping every boy and girl achieve the highest degree of development of which he or she is capable in and through the life of a society. Education is primarily regarded in terms of growth of soul, mind and body. It is exploratory and creative, rather than a mere passive receptivity. It negates conditioning the student to tribal settings, it acquires a universal application.[28]

In effect the Education Committee was arguing that the educational process must be based on broader objectives than Stark was advocating. It saw education as an endeavor to teach all students how to engage in fulfilling activity, to gain new ideas, to have a positive perception of themselves, to eliminate the illusions of the narrow goals of the educative process, and to avoid the disillusionment of what was prescribed from above.

Stark chose to ignore the thinking among some whites that education for Africans must place due emphasis upon two essential elements of human existence — the potential to give everyone the intellectual ability to see himself or herself in relation to a larger social order, and the opportunity to train for a respectable career in the pursuit of one's objectives.[29] The Education Committee was aware that throughout the world, philosophy and intellectual growth were high-sounding terms, often elusive and hard to define in specific educational and social settings. Stark certainly wanted to attach his own definitions of these terms to his philosophy, especially the relationship between the school and tribal life.

But what Stark believed to be a knowledge of the African condition — the fact that even in its rudiments education enables the child to gain power to control his or her own destiny, to understand the difference between fact and fiction, between what is good and what is bad, to acquire a perspective, a sense of values — was the major reason why he said in 1936 that education in the hands of the primitive, meaning the powerless Africans, was a dangerous instrument of agitation.

Stark also preferred to neglect the principle that the fundamental objective of education is to place in the student's mind ideas of what things really are and how he or she can interact with the world. Any education that does this is a success, and any education that fails to do this is a failure. Stark's philosophy resulted in an education that was less than successful because it was too restricted to fall within the universal definition of its purpose. That the Education Committee of 1943 also took issue with Stark's philosophy that practical training and basic literacy were the means to train the Africans to acquire character as defined by Western criteria is an important development. Stark was unequivocal in arguing that to meet these criteria the Africans must demonstrate absolute obedience to colonial authority, living a life of basic simplicity, relegating political activity to the white man, and accepting without any question the kind of education the white man, through the colonial government, said was good for them.

In disagreeing with Stark, the Education Committee argued:

> A man's mind, his integrity, his sense of responsibility and his values as a citizen depend on his having a standard of conduct with which the educational process enables him to understand his sense of rightness and justice. In a totalitarian state he is not allowed to judge these matters for himself. The controlling authority lags down the standard and blind obedience and blind loyalty are required. Thus, the burden of moral responsibility is placed on him unfairly.[30]

There is absolutely no doubt that the Education Committee recognized these as conditions which controlled the education and the life of the Africans under Stark's philosophy.

Three years later, in February, 1946, the Methodist Church joined the Education Committee in criticizing Stark's philosophy and policy, saying:

> We believe that a satisfactory educational policy awaits a clear enunciation of principles regarding the Africans' place in social, economic and political life of the country and that the formation of definite lines of development by the Africans so that they reach the full and unrestricted citizenship which we believe is unquestionably their right.[31]

There is no question also that the Methodist Church had recognized the weakness inherent in Stark's philosophy and was urging him to re-consider it. The question was: Would he agree? But whether or not he would agree is really beside the point. The point is that he could not continue to have everyone believe that he was pursuing a policy which meant the development of African education. That little white lie or myth, had been recognized for what it really was, a farce.

Summary and Conclusion

There are three disturbing things about Stark's philosophy of African education. The first is that the African people might have recognized the handicap under which they labored, but when it came to practical reality, they found that their lives were bound by a complex of colonial structure beyond their control. This was the beginning of the rise of their political consciousness. Stark's philosophy, regardless of the gallant efforts he made to prove the contrary, indirectly aided in that process.

The second thing is that in formulating his philosophy of education for Africans, Stark was true to the traditional colonial attitude. The system of education that he established after Jowitt resigned provided what appeared to be a definite and irrefutable knowledge of what constituted education for Africans. He failed to recognize that in emphasizing practical training, the Africans were oppressed physically and intellectually. He did this because he believed that the colonial condition would perpetuate itself, and that there was no need for any other form of education for Africans. Basing the formulation and the implementation of his policy on this belief had a special appeal to Huggins and his government. That is why Stark remained in office for 20 years.

The third disturbing thing about Stark's philosophy of education for Africans was that his talking about the capability of Western education as an instrument of conditioning the Africans to their tribal settings meant that he was totally out of touch with reality. Granted that the Africans might not have wanted to acquire the basic elements of a colonial culture; nonetheless, they did not ask for the kind of education that would enable them to relate better to tribal condition. This suggests, therefore, that Stark saw this reaction as an instrument of subjecting them to a more oppressive form of political domination. In Chapter 4 the effects of implementing Stark's philosophy on both African education and life, as well as on broader aspects of national life, will be presented.

Notes

1. George Stark, The Annual Report of the Acting Director of Native Development, 1934, p. 1.
2. Ibid. p. 3
3. Southern Rhodesia, Advisory Board for Native Development. Salisbury (Harare): Government Printer, 1933, p. 4
4. Southern Rhodesia Christian Conference, Annual Report, 1934.
5. Harold Jowitt, The Annual Report of the Director of Native Education, 1930, p. 12.
6. When this author was in primary school at Old Mutare School, Stark came there during a tour of the area. He was of a modest physical appearance and severe facial expression, suggesting the personality of a troubled man.
7. George Stark, The Annual Report of the Acting Director of Native Development, 1934, p. 1.
8. Harold Jowitt, The Annual Report of the Director of Native Education, 1933, p. 6.
9. George Stark, writing an inspection report of Masasa School, in Harold Jowitt, The Annual Report of the Director of Native Development, 1930, p. 3.
10. George Stark, The Annual Report of the Director of Native Education, 1935, p. 18.
11. Ibid. p. 19.
12. Ibid. p. 20.
13. Ibid. p. 21.
14. Ibid. p. 23
15. Ibid. p. 24
16. The Report of the Land Commission, Morris Carter, Chairman, 1925, p. 5. In the Zimbabwe National Archives.
17. George Stark, The Annual Report of the Director of Native Education, 1935, p. 19.
18. George Stark, The Annual Report of the Director of Native Education, 1936, p. 13.
19. Ibid. p. 15.
20. Ibid. p. 22.
21. Southern Rhodesia Christian Conference: A Resolution on Native Education, 1937. Stark also records this resolution in his annual report for 1937, p. 13.
22. See Chapter 4 of this volume for details.
23. George Stark, The Annual Report of the Director of Native Education, 1938, p. 14.
24. Ibid. p. 15.
25. Ibid., p. 16.
26. George Stark, The Annual Report of the Director of Native Education, 1943, p. 125.
27. George Stark, The Annual Report of the Director of Native Education, 1938, p. 17.
28. Southern Rhodesia, The Report of the Education Committee, 1943, p. 52. By courtesy of the Zimbabwe National Archives.
29. Ibid. p. 53.
30. Ibid.. p. 54.
31. The Methodist Church, The Waddilove Manifesto: The Education Policy of the Methodist Church, a statement asking the government to design a new educational policy for Africans, February 8-9, 1946. In the Old Mutare Methodist Archives.

4
The Effect of Implementing Stark's Philosophy: Assuring African Progress or Serving Government Interests?

The Native people, like people everywhere, must work out their own salvation.
—George Stark, 1934

The Administrative Structure of African Education

While Stark formulated his philosophy of African education consistent with larger government objectives, he believed that he lacked the legal basis to implement it in a way that would not invoke criticism from the missionaries or from those who disagreed with it. But because he enjoyed the total confidence and support of his superiors, he had little difficulty in persuading Huggins to create such a basis.

This is why, as soon as Stark's appointment was confirmed in 1935, the Huggins administration promulgated Government Notice Number 177/35, by which Stark was appointed chief administrative officer to coordinate all levels of native education.[1] Not only did the government notice give Stark power to formulate and implement his educational policies, it also gave him authority to cooperate with the Department of Native Affairs in the general conduct of its business. This established a precedent that the right-wing Rhodesia Front government, led by Ian Smith, used effectively from 1964 to 1979.

It is important to remember that there were two essential components of Stark's philosophy of education for Africans. The first had to do with practical training; the second was to prepare Africans to live under tribal conditions never leaving that environment to interact with an urban one. Throughout the 20 years he was in office, Stark never compromised these aspects of his philosophy. Any educational policy he designed was intended to promote them. That in Huggins was a strong and reliable partner helps to explain the length of his term of office.

In 1939, in a move clearly intended to give Stark more power than he needed, Huggins issued Government Notice Number 358/39, repealing Government Notice Number 676 of 1929, and allocated $22,800 to formulate and implement Stark's policy.[2] From then on, Stark's power was absolute and consolidated. He was more powerful and more influential than the chief native commissioner. Granted the legal basis that he needed to implement his philosophy, Stark was ready to do as he pleased and play the game according to his own rules. What he said, was done without question. His word was law. It was a rebirth of the old way of thinking, a reincarnation of Keigwin. The character of African education was at his mercy. He had become absolute in every way.

The Effect of Implementing Stark's Philosophy: Its Three Essential Components

Stark's careful choice of three essential components through which to implement his philosophy demonstrates the extent of his belief in the effect of that philosophy on the character of African education. These components were: the curriculum structure, supervision of schools, and training of African personnel. Stark regarded all three as closely related, and therefore wanted to see an integrated approach to the implementation of his philosophy. Let us take one component at a time and discuss how its implementation was related to his philosophy and how it affected African education, Stark style.

Curriculum: Drastic Reduction of Courses

In accordance with the requirements of Education Ordinance of 1899, as amended in 1901, 1902, 1907, and 1912, Stark made sure that African education extended to 40 hours of instruction per week. He ordered that more than half this time be devoted to industrial training because "the Native must not be trained to enter into competition with the European[3] artisan."[4] Practical training extended over eight years, from Sub standard A to Standard VI. Stark made sure that each class took courses spread over the eight-year period, beginning with elementary courses in building, agriculture, carpentry, domestic work, and general construction. In 1940 he ordered a change in the admission criteria to require, *inter alia*, that Domboshawa and Tjolotjo be only for those who wanted to take a three-year course beyond Standard Vi in one of the areas of study.

The three-year courses offered at Domboshawa and Tjolotjo resulted from Stark's view that:

> A Native who has completed a course in building is not an efficient builder, as efficiency is reckoned amongst European artisans. No claim can be made by this Department that any Native trained at any of the Native schools will, as a result of his training in carpentry, building, or agriculture, be efficient in the creation of buildings required by Europeans.[5]

If there had been any doubt about the effect Stark had intended in implementing his philosophy of African education, it was now evident that he wanted to remove it at the beginning of his tenure. This statement reveals what Stark really intended the policy of practical training to accomplish. The effect of this training program on African education was what Stark wanted as an outcome of the curriculum he put in place: preparing Africans to readjust to tribal settings. However, one must not conclude that Stark was a callous colonial official out to oppress Africans but, rather, that he tried to bring about change in the system in order to improve it. But what actually resulted may not be regarded as an improvement, but as a curtailment.

In arguing that the curriculum in African schools was an outcome of a "definite policy of the Department to give instruction in various courses of value to the Native pupil living under tribal conditions,"[6] Stark was emphasizing the importance of preparing Africans to live in tribal settings. He does not appear to have been worried by the contradictory situation his rhetoric represented: How would the Africans be trained to function as cheap laborers and at the same time be conditioned to tribal settings? By 1936, Stark outlined new curricular guidelines that included instruction in literacy in order to enhance the teaching of practical courses. He also demanded an introduction of new courses, such as leather work, as "of great service to Native progress."[7] In demanding that additional buildings be erected at Domboshawa and Tjolotjo to accommodate expected expansion, Stark was precluding any possible development of a balanced educational program of industrial training and academic education for Africans.

To ensure that the curriculum in all African schools was being carried out as he demanded, Stark ordered that missionary superintendents supervise the teachers thoroughly, and allowed no discretion in making adjustments to suit the demands of the conditions: "The schools depend to a large extent on the knowledge and enthusiasm of the superintendents. Weak superintendents have weak schools regardless of the qualifications of the teacher."[8] For all his claimed knowledge of the essential elements of the curriculum in African schools, Stark did not realize that with only a few years of education, the Africans in urban areas would create problems beyond his ability to solve. Thus, in 1942, he was forced to admit, "The problem of the education of Native children is most acute in the large locations of Salisbury [Harare] and Bulawayo."[9] Stark had opposed a large number of Africans' moving into urban areas and therefore had formulated a philosophy that called for an education which would condition them to tribal settings.

Unfortunately while Stark recognized the existence of serious problems created by the implementation of his philosophy, his efforts to solve them yielded limited results. The rapid increase in the number of Africans moving into urban areas was a development that he regretted, but one that was made necessary by the expanding industries which needed cheap labor. Thus, Stark was caught in a dilemma created by his own philosophy. His emphasis of literacy and practical training as essential objectives in African education suggests his limited ability to recognize the rapid changes taking place in urban communities. His ignorance that the emergence of this serious problem was the beginning of a national crisis was perhaps the reason for his unwillingness to consider any alternative educational policy.

In seeking to implement his philosophy of African education relative to curricular structure, Stark seemed to neglect an important fact: that at any level of universal education, the curriculum manifests the concept of equal educational opportunity because the latter is considered to be a national asset. It was virtually impossible for him to recognize this essential principle of the educational process because he was too much a part of the old thinking — a traditional colonial attitude that made it difficult for him to see the Africans from any other perspective. Stark found it hard to appreciate that the curriculum should be designed to promote freedom of inquiry as a distinctive quality of human intellect and as an essential feature of the learning process. It never occurred to him that the kind of curriculum he demanded for African schools would foster an environment of cultural bias and racial conflict, because he viewed the educational process from a racial perspective.

There is yet another important consideration that Stark seems to have neglected relative to the kind of the curriculum he demanded for African schools: that curricular content should meet the occupational, physical, spiritual, intellectual, and social needs of the students. In universal education, the curriculum is regarded as a means of developing the learner's potential and promoting his or her interests in an unrestricted manner. Therefore, the curriculum, in universal education, is intended to be far more important than it was in Stark's definition. For this reason, the Education Committee of 1943 criticized his philosophy of education for Africans, with special reference to his ideas on the curriculum. It listed the essential components of a good curriculum:

> Language, religion, history, geography, mathematics, science, music, art, handicraft, physical education are important in any school. They should give pupils a knowledge of the natural laws which operate in the universe and of their application to society. The resulting curriculum cannot be imposed.[10]

The Education Committee's conclusion about the weaknesses of Stark's ideas on the curriculum reveals that he failed to design it in such a way as to allow Africans to have a thorough knowledge of the methods of thought process and inquiry necessary to reveal the influence of human achievement and institutional evolution on the human condition and civilization. Stark was a zealous government official who believed he was carrying out his duty in order to preserve the social status quo.

Further, the development of a curriculum consistent with the aspirations of Africans would have entailed broader objectives, intended to assist the students in acquiring a body of knowledge in a number of important areas of human endeavor, than the limitations Stark's policy imposed. In such a setting, students, both male and female, would have been given equal opportunity to engage in critical thinking through the learning process. Industrial arts would have replaced practical training in order to allow for creative learning and recreational activity. These are the realities the Education Committee of 1943 took into consideration in criticizing Stark's ideas of the curriculum: "The result is that a student's knowledge of both himself and the conditions that control his life are fragmented. There is the danger of incoherence, of a major social conflict in the future."[11] For the Education Committee to expect Stark and the government he represented to understand the importance of this truth was to expect them to appreciate the harmful effects of colonialism. This had not been done before in the history of educational policy for Africans in Zimbabwe, and Stark would not be the first to try it. This refusal to do so set the stage for a major national crisis to emerge beginning in 1946. That the curriculum was a major cause of that crisis is demonstrated by the critical events which began to unfold with the formation of the radical City Youth League in 1956 and the African National Congress in 1957.

Supervision by Inspectors: Ascertaining Wise Spending?

Jowitt's interpretation of the provisions of the Education Ordinance of 1899 was that the inspectors of schools were appointed to assist in the development of education. He believed that a team of four inspectors, one for each province, was quite sufficient. He was careful to instruct his inspectors not to be judgmental in their evaluation of the work the schools were doing, but to be helpful, to offer constructive ideas and suggestions rather than to be critical, to consult rather than to confront: to accentuate the positive rather than emphasize the negative.[12]

But as soon as Stark took office, he not only demanded an increase in the number of inspectors, he also assigned them an entirely new role: rigorous enforcement of his policies. Within a few years the inspectors acquired a highly negative reputation among African students and teachers alike. They portrayed themselves as high-ranking government officials out to prove they had the power to order African educators around.[13] They showed no respect for either the teachers' innovative ideas or the students' learning initiative.

Unwilling to trust the work the missionary superintendents were doing, Stark instructed his inspectors to carry out their inspection responsibility with a show of authority and power, to make sure that his policy was implemented as he had designed it. When, in 1937, one inspector reported, ''Teaching is becoming stereotyped and only a matter of academic interest,''[14] Stark quickly convened a joint conference of the missionaries and his inspectors to discuss the problem and to resolve it, giving the impression that the schools were violating his policy by emphasizing academic education instead of practical training. In characteristic fashion, Stark went on the offensive and ordered his inspectors to find ''ways and means of alleviating the situation through a drastic reduction of the curriculum and of the number of special courses.''[15] Needless to say, the academic components of the curriculum were what he ordered eliminated. The missionary superintendents were given no chance to explain the reasons for their effort to allow a limited number of academic courses into the curriculum.

It was clear that Stark wanted to prove that supervision of African schools by inspectors of his department meant an improvement of the conduct of the educational process. To strengthen his argument he quoted the report of one of them: ''On all industrial work there is noticeable a greater enthusiasm and a very much improved attitude among Native students to do their work. There is less of the lackadaisical attitude which was unpleasantly obvious previously.''[16] Stark concluded that this ''increased the usefulness and efficiency of the school and has unquestionably a beneficial influence on the labor situation and on Native life in the villages.''[17] It is easy to see that his comment was the result of the action of his inspcctors.

With the promulgation of Government Notice Number 358 in 1939, stating, ''Subject to financial provision being available, it shall be competent for the Minister to authorize the establishment of undenominational primary schools in any industrialized areas. These schools shall be controlled by the Department of Native Education,''[18] Stark felt that the additional responsibility to supervise all schools was a positive response to his policy and an expression of confidence in the work that his inspectors were doing. Therefore, he was very careful to make sure that all the schools offered a curriculum which would enable the graduates to function well in the industries near them.

In the procedures Stark outlined in 1940 for the inspection of schools, the missionary superintendents were required to visit each school under their care four times a year and to remain there for the full day's session, thoroughly inspecting each teacher's work.[19] The criteria Stark outlined included the following: Does the teacher possess the ability to impart knowledge of simple industrial skills to his students? Does he keep records of all the projects in the school: agricultural, handicrafts, building, and so on? Does the teacher have the general character all teachers should possess? Does the teacher show respect for those in authority over him? The success of any school was determined by the inspector's opinion of how well it did in teaching industrial courses. The inspector for Mutare, for example, reported in 1944:

> Industrial work, especially agriculture, has improved in this school. The teachers, too, are becoming interested in good crops and good tidy gardens. Vegetables are becoming more popular. I believe that this is one of the best forms of educational work being related to the lives of the Natives in the villages.[20]

By 1945, when the policy of practical training was being questioned, Stark sought to improve it by not allowing his inspectors to consider academic courses in the curriculum. Therefore in a report of his inspection visit to Waddilove in that year, one inspector wrote:

> Here practical work is conducted on a farm of 150 acres. The principal operations include animal husbandry and dairying, farm crop production, vegetable gardening, tree planting, and fruit growing. All students are doing building with related woodwork and thatching, metal work, cement work, well-sinking, stumping and similar operations. The pupils are keen on their work.[21]

Nowhere does this report mention the need for a balance between practical training and academic education. It is not surprising that in 1946, meeting at the same Waddilove School, the Methodist Church convened a special conference to discuss Stark's educational policy and to criticize it heavily for placing too much emphasis on practical training at the expense of good academic education.[22]

By 1948, Stark felt that his policy was so successful he wanted to introduce the next phase of his philosophy of relating the school to tribal life. He therefore ordered that rural Africans be involved in school projects relevant to their life-style. He cited what he claimed was a successful experiment in Mzingwane Area, of which one inspector wrote: "A very successful innovation this year was the African Vegetable Garden Association, consisting of Natives from the nearby reserve. All post-standard VI agricultural people attended these meetings."[23] But amid this euphoria and claimed success in the implementation of his philosophy, Stark revealed a serious contradiction in his professional action. The effect that he wanted to see as a successful implementation of his policy, strengthening of the ties between school and tribal life, was not what happened. In 1948, the principal of Domboshawa explained why:

> The number of students offering for training in industrial courses has been very disappointing. The reason for this is that pupils who have completed a two-year post-standard VI building or carpentry course cannot command a much higher salary than those in the general labor market.[24]

This is what the policy of practical training was designed to do and Stark knew it.

With all these signals, and suggestions that the days of practical training as the only form of viable education for Africans were over, Stark was still unwilling to face the reality that he was behind the times. Instead, he instructed his inspectors to insist on practical training and industrial courses as if nothing was happening. To demonstrate her loyalty to Stark, one female inspector of women's work wrote after inspecting Beit Home Craft School for African women in 1950:

> Practical work here is of a very good standard and is being carried out in such a way that it will be easy to carry it on at their homes in the Reserves. The more of these schools that are established, the better will be for the Native Reserves and the labor supply.[25]

Stark used this report to justify his request for an increase in the number of inspectors. In 1951, he argued:

> Whilst industrial work still does not receive in all schools the place it should have in the curriculum, from many districts come reports of a high standard reached and a greater stress laid on practical training and agriculture, which, after all, will always be the main occupation of the Natives in rural areas.[26]

When, due to increasing criticism of his policy, the request for an increase in the number of inspectors was denied, Stark felt that he had lost the power and the influence he once exercised, and took the opportunity to express his displeasure with the way things were going: "Without the constant checking up by the inspectors it cannot be ascertained whether the money spent on a school is being used wisely or is being wasted."[27] Like Keigwin, Stark knew that the end of his power and influence was near.

One sees two things in Stark's efforts to implement his philosophy of African education through the curriculum and through the supervision of schools by inspectors. The first is that there is no evidence to suggest that African education improved as a result. Instead, as time went on, there was even more doubt than in 1934 that industrial training was a viable education. His admission that the Africans with three-year training were not much better than ordinary laborers, and the criticism from the Education Committee of 1943 and from the Methodist Church in 1946, suggested that Stark was pursuing his policy not to assure African progress but to serve the interests of the colonial government .

The second thing one sees is that Stark deliberately refused to acknowledge the fact that conditions of 1953 were quite different from those of 1934. His refusal to consider the possibility that Africans needed an education better than simple practical training shows the extent of his rigidity and unwillingness to face reality. Even the denial of his request for an increase in the number of inspectors in 1953 did not mean anything to him. In that same year, Huggins was replaced as prime minister by Garfield Todd, a former missionary from New Zealand, an event that spelled the end of Stark's government service.

Training African Personnel: Eliminating Indifference?

The third and final component of Stark's implementation of his philosophy of African education was the strategy he used to train the African personnel. As soon as his appointment was confirmed, Stark explained how important this was to the success of his policy:

> The training of teachers holds an important place in the educational system for Natives. In their training the stress is laid, not merely on methods of teaching, but upon the necessity for the teacher to be imbued with a high sense of responsibility to the whole community in which he resides. It is emphasized that the teacher who regards his work merely as teaching of the three R's has no proper vision of the greatness of his task.[28]

There is no doubt that Stark wanted the African teachers to believe that just as the laborer was worthy of his hire, so they must be trained to teach industrial courses as the only route to the salvation of their people.

In arguing, that "The industrial training given to the teachers shows a marked improvement in the employment of better workers,"[29] Stark wanted the colonial business community to believe that its members could count on him to formulate and implement a policy for the training of Africans capable of meeting their labor needs.

In order to practice binding ties between the school and tribal life, Stark formulated a policy of training teachers capable of teaching courses in what Keigwin defined in 1920 as village industries. This had no relevance to traditional African life. The courses included agriculture, handicrafts, and other simple industrial activities. Stark advanced his reason for avoiding advanced training courses for Africans, saying, "However valuable any advanced courses may be to the teachers, they do not facilitate the teaching of suitable village industries."[30]

Another important aspect of implementing Stark's philosophy of African education was his efforts to train chiefs to function in cooperation with village teachers. He ordered them to go to Domboshawa to undergo training so that they would understand, appreciate, and cooperate in any school activity related to village life. He argued in 1935: "This experiment of training chiefs is an effort to educate Native public opinion to appreciate the aims of the school, to eliminate the indifference which is a disturbing factor of the school process."[31] Therefore, Domboshawa and Tjolotjo remained the two major centers for training African personnel until the end of the colonial government in 1979. As under Keigwin, both schools were at the center stage of Stark's program. The following table shows, at five-year intervals, total enrollment for each school during the years Stark was in office.

Enrollment At Domboshawa And Tjolotjo Compared, 1933-1953

Year	*Domboshawa*	*Tjolotjo*	*Total*
1933	278	123	401
1938	266	208	474
1943	288	227	515
1948	302	263	565
1953	294	250	544

Source: The Annual Reports of the Director of Native Education, 1933-1954

The fact that there were seven church-related schools[32] offering industrial courses in agriculture, building, carpentry, and leather work seems to have convinced Stark that he was pursuing a good educational policy, and he therefore refused to consider any other curricular elements. But by 1953, Domboshawa and Tjolotjo, the brain-children of Herbert Keigwin, and George Stark's symbols of power, were beginning to write his political epitaph, just as they had for Keigwin.

Another important aspect of Stark's philosophy that he implemented to ensure that the African schools were related to tribal settings was what he called vacation courses. Stark demanded that teachers attend courses during vacation and ordered inspectors to teach them. He explained the reason for demanding that teachers attend these courses:

> Vacation courses are essential for Native teachers who are teaching in areas where cultural associations are restricted. It is a drain on the inspector's physical and mental resources to use school vacation to teach courses to teachers when he has had a heavy term conducting inspections. But his reward should be in the response of the teachers.[33]

Stark's major concern in this regard was to make sure that what he called "cultural associations" was a redefinition of relating African education to tribal settings. Stark could not see the development of African education from any other perspective.

In order to ensure that the training of African personnel, in all its dimensions, served the purpose for which he formulated his policies, Stark modified the plan that Jowitt put in place in 1929, the training of Jeanes teachers.[34] Jowitt's original plan, like his original plan for inspectors, was to train Jeanes teachers so that they were adequately prepared to help less qualified teachers improve their overall performance. Jowitt saw this as a genuine attempt to overcome some serious problems related to his efforts to improve the village schools. The criteria he used to select those to be trained as Jeanes teachers included personal commitment to the educational advancement of Africans, reasonable academic preparation, and good character. Their original function included helping teachers improve their effectiveness in motivating their students to engage in purposeful educational activity.

As soon as Stark's appointment was confirmed, he convened a conference, held from May 27 to June 7, 1935, of the Jeanes teachers already serving, to reorient them to his requirements. He decided that "There should be no candidates accepted for training in 1935 in order to consider the value of Jeanes training and make decisions regarding any courses which may be held in the future."[35] Fearing that the Jeanes teachers were loyal to Jowitt, and that they resented his attitude toward them, Stark expressed concern that they might "not do good community work"[36] under his leadership. He went on to argue that experience showed it was that students did not do well to adjust to conditions under which they lived, but that the attitude and the strategy of their teachers made a difference.

The encouraging feature of the Jeanes teachers under Jowitt was their successful contact with an educational environment, which aided their efforts while they were still in training. Jowitt had impressed upon them the need to develop skills to reach out and help those lacking basic literacy in addition to their regular work of helping the teachers. This approach had a positive influence on the relationship between them. But under Stark the role of the Jeanes teachers was modified to focus on helping both teachers and students to undertake an effective practical training program. As Stark saw it, "The Native people, like people everywhere, must work out their own salvation."[37] Given the nature of the conditions controlling the Africans, this is a truism of sorts.

What really worried Stark about the Jeanes teachers under Jowitt was what he perceived as a weakness: that "The Jeanes teachers may be highly trained as individuals, each of whom is an expert in teaching methods. But unless each can arouse the people with whom he will deal to respond to the suggestions which he may make towards a better way of village life, he will be useless.[38]" To make sure that this did not happen, Stark required that each Jeanes teacher understand fully that his responsibility was to implement official policy first, and to help teachers second. In this regard, he altered the role of the Jeanes teachers from assisting teachers to becoming agents for the implementation of his philosophy and policy. The following table shows the distribution of Jeanes teachers in 1936.

Male		**Male**		**Female**	
School	*No. of Jeanes Teachers*	*School*	*No. of Jeanes Teachers*	*School*	*No. of Jeanes Teachers*
Mt. Selinda	1	Nyadiri	1	Mt. Selinda	1
Chikore	2	Old Mutare	2	St. Augustine's	1
St. Augustine's	1	Sinoia	1	Matopo	1
St. David's	1	Epworth	1	Makumbe	1
St. Mary's	1	Chibero	1	Gutu	1
Wanenzi	1	Tegwani	1	Morgenster	1
Jichidza	2	Selukwe	1	Hope Fountain	1
Pamushana	1	Kwenda	1	Inyati	2
Makumbe	1	Triashill	1	Dombodema	3
Morgenster	1	St. Barbara	1	Mutambara	1
Chibi	1	Kutama	1	Mrewa	1
Gutu	1	Empandeni	1	Nyadiri	1
Hope Fountain	1	Harare	1	Epworth	1
Dombodema	2	Gwanda	1	Waddilove	1
Shangani	1			Ingwenya	1
Total	18	Total	15	Total	19

There is no question that Stark firmly believed in the colonial philosophy that "If any group of people remains adamant to all forms of teaching, it is impossible for any progress to be made,"[39] but his definition of progress was quite different from the universal definition. This was why he ordered the Jeanes teachers become his agents in implementing his policy. If the Africans would not be aroused to take an active interest in this kind of development, Stark believed that old-fashioned colonial paternalism must come into play. Therefore, the experiment that began under Jowitt took a new twist under Stark.

The question now was: How effective were the Jeanes teachers under Stark? To find an answer, one needs to see how effective they were under Jowitt. In 1932, the inspector for Matabeleland was so impressed with their work that he wrote: "The effectiveness of the Jeanes teachers in improving the village schools has been well assured judging by the results achieved this year. They have revolutionized the whole of the school life."[40]

In 1938, Stark himself admitted, "There is a difference of opinion as to the value of the work of the Jeanes teachers."[41] He did not mention that the reason for what he considered a controversy was his own attitude toward them. It is therefore really not surprising that by 1943, the Jeanes teachers program, which Jowitt had used to improve African education, but which Stark used as part of the administrative structure to implement his philosophy, came to an end.

Summary and Conclusion

This chapter shows that in implementing his philosophy of education for Africans, Stark was motivated by two major considerations. The first is that he wanted to demonstrate that he was a true colonial loyalist who would go to any length to succeed in preparing Africans to serve as efficient laborers. We have quoted statement after statement to show that this was what he wanted to accomplish. There is also evidence to support this conclusion in the kind of the curriculum he designed, the work of his inspectors, and the training of African personnel.

All these components demonstrate the coherence of his philosophy. The question is: Did it achieve the desired result? The evidence we have presented in this chapter leads to the conclusion that it did not. Then why did he pursue it? Because he thought it would work, and because he was a colonialist of the old school, he did not recognize the essential change in conditions that should have brought a corresponding change which would have motivated the formulation and implementation of his educational policy for Africans. But to expect an ardent colonial official to engage in this form of exercise would be to expect too much.

The second consideration is Stark's belief that the school, as far as it was related to Africans, must give meaning to the tribal condition. In other words, the school must strengthen tribal settings. His attempts to train African chiefs and to reorient the Jeanes teachers, and his hesitation to train new ones, demonstrate how he remained convinced of his philosophy. One must conclude that the overall effect of implementing his philosophy did not translate into African advancement, but into serving the interests of the colonial establishment.

In all that he did, Stark remained an ardent colonialist who saw the education of Africans from the traditional colonial perspective. The ultimate effect of implementing his philosophy was that in failing to assure the educational progress of Africans, he hurt the interests of the colonial establishment he was trying to serve. Chapter 5 will review how the alliance between Stark and Godfrey Huggins became a major problem, not a solution, for African education.

Notes

1. Southern Rhodesia, Government Notice Number 177/35, 1935.
2. Southern Rhodesia, Government Notice Number 358/39, 1939.
3. In British colonial traditions, ''European'' meant anyone who was white. In the same way ''Native'' meant anyone who was black. However, in 1962, ''African'' was substituted for ''Native'' because the Africans resented the negative connotation in which the whites used the latter.
4. George Stark, The Annual Report of the Director of Native Education, 1935, p. 13.
5. Ibid., p. 14.
6. Ibid., p. 16.
7. Ibid., p. 15.
8. George Stark, The Annual Report of the Director of Native Education, 1937, p. 16.
9. George Stark, The Annual Report of the Director of Native Education, 1942, p. 70.
10. Southern Rhodesia, The Report of the Education Committee, 1943, p. 60
11. Ibid., p. 65.
12. Harold Jowitt, The Annual Report of the Director of Native Education, 1929.
13. The author clearly remembers how J. H. Farquhur, C. S. Davies, David Stewart, Gerald Gardener, for example, were feared by African students and teachers alike in the 1950s when they came to inspect the schools he was attending in eastern Zimbabwe.
14. George Stark, The Annual Report of the Director of Native Education, 1937, p. 16.
15. Ibid., p. 18.
16. George Stark, The Annual Report of the Director of Native Education, 1938, p. 17.
17. Ibid., p. 18.
18. Southern Rhodesia, Government Notice Number 358, 1939, Section 44.
19. George Stark, The Annual Report of the Director of Native Education, 1944, p. 177.
20. Ibid., p.178.
21. George Stark, The Annual Report of the Director of Native Education, 1945, p. 226.
22. The Methodist Church, The Waddilove Manifesto: The Education Policy of the Methodist Church. February 8-9, 1946, discussed in Chapter 2 of this volume. 23. George Stark, The Annual Report of the Director of Native Education, 1948, p. 35.
24. The Principal of Domboshawa, A Special Report, 1948. In the Zimbabwe National Archives.
25. George Stark, The Annual Report of the Director of Native Education, 1950, p. 35.
26. George Stark, The Annual Report of the Director of Native Education, 1951, p. 24.
27. George Stark, The Annual Report of the Director of Native Education, 1953, p. 36.
28. George Stark, The Annual Report of the Director of Native Education, 1935, p. 16.
29. Ibid., p. 17.
30. Ibid., p. 17.
31. Ibid.., P. 20.
32. These were Chikore, Waddilove, Mt. Selinda, Empandeni, Inyati, Tegwani (which the author attended as a secondary student from 1956 to 1957), and Inyazura.
33. George Stark, The Annual Report of the Director of Native Education, 1953, p. 34.
34. Teachers who were trained under this scheme became itinerant master teachers known as Jeanes teachers, named in honor of Anna T. Jeanes, a philanthropist from Philadelphia who had given money for the educational development of blacks in the U.S..S. South. The Carnegie Corporation assumed the responsibility of administering the financial aspects of the Jeanes training programs in a number of countries in Africa, including colonial Zimbabwe, beginning in 1929.
35. George Stark, The Annual Report of the Director of Native Education, 1935, p. 9.
36. Ibid., p. 10.
37. George Stark, The Annual Report of the Director of Native Education, 1934, p. 9.
38. Ibid., p. 11.
39. Ibid., p. 19.

40. Harold Jowitt, The Annual Report of the Director of Native Education, 1932, p. 11.
41. George Stark, The Annual Report of the Director of Native Education, 1938, p. 22.

Photo Essay

Cecil John Rhodes, the architect of British colonial empire in Africa. "The Natives are children, we must treat them as a subject race as long as they remain in their state of barbarism." Photo courtesy of the National Archives of Zimbabwe.

George Duthie, Inspector of Schools, 1901. ''If there is a development of any other industry for Natives, so much the better.'' Photo courtesy of the National Archives of Zimbabwe.

Tegwani School for Africans, 1903. ''Education for Natives must equip them to live in their own conditions of life.'' George Stark, 1938. Photo courtesy of the National Archives of Zimbabwe.

Godfrey Huggins, prime minister 1933-52. "The Native must not be allowed to invade the shores of civilization." Photo courtesy of the National Archives of Zimbabwe.

George Stark, Director of Native Education, 1935-54. "The fundamental objective in African education must be to make an effort to bind more closely the ties between the school and tribal life." Photo courtesy of the National Archives of Zimbabwe.

The author as high school student at Tegwani Secondary School, 1957. "Education is an essential tool for gaining a foothold in a competitive world." Photo by M. Ndubiwa.

The author, right, and a friend, Oliver Musuka, as primary teachers, 1961. ''Training of teachers holds an important place in Native Education.'' Photo by S. Sigauke.

An African child working for a white farmer, 1940. "The Natives must be taught habits of discipline." Photo courtesy of E. T. Brown.

Christopher Magadza with his first slate, 1941. "The policy of raising the mass is preferred to the advancement of a few." Photo courtesy of E. T. Brown.

The installation of Chief Nyakunu Zimunya, 1968. "Native chiefs must be trained to cooperate in school activity related to the village." Photo by the author.

A. M. Mungazi (the author's father), 1961. "The fundamental objective of education is to place in the mind of the student ideas of what things really are." Photo by L. Mutema.

African students in nurses' training school at Nyadiri Methodist Hospital, 1954. "Educated Natives are reluctant to undertake strenuous manual labor." Photo from Methodist Information Services, Old Mutare.

African teachers and preachers, 1965. From left to right: Martin Chiza, John Kaemer, Benjamin Jambga, Caled Mukasa, William Buwu, Lovemore Nyanungo, Patrick Matsikenyire, Kenneth Chikwinya. ''Let our teaching be such that our pupils go out of our schools as ambassadors of light.'' Photo by the author.

Chief Munhuwepai Mangwende of the Mangwende Reserve, 1937-60. "Under the chief's leadership the Mangwende Rural Council became a shining example of a progressive organization." Photo courtesy of the National Archives of Zimbabwe.

5
The Alliance Between Huggins and Stark: A Major Problem in Education for Africans

It would be outrageous to give the Native a so-called political partnership and equal educational opportunity when he is likely to ruin himself as a result. — Godfrey Huggins, 1954.

Stark's Reversal of Something of Suggestive Value

When Stark recognized in 1934 that his appointment as acting director of native education was received with considerable skepticism among the missionaries, he was, in effect, admitting that they regarded him as part of the problem they believed African education was going to experience. The lack of trust in him was mainly due to the belief that he was going to reverse the progress Jowitt had made. Stark himself recognized it,[1] and events were to prove that their apprehensions were justified.

There is evidence to suggest that Stark and his associates in the colonial hierarchy did not support the direction which Jowitt had defined for African education because, as Jowitt said in 1929: "We shall strive in our system to develop the potential capacities of the Native into dynamic abilities, to keep in touch with what is happening elsewhere of suggestive value. We have to maintain racial affinities instead of creating a gulf."[2] This view was a complete departure from the traditional colonial attitude toward Africans, and Stark and his colleagues therefore worried about the consequences. Thus, in the pursuit of his own policies radically different from those of Jowitt, Stark reversed this thing of suggestive value.

There is no question that Stark saw Jowitt's policy as a move toward providing equal educational opportunity to Africans in an environment of conflict. In the context of the colonial setting, this could not be done and still claim the superiority of the white man. If no claim of white superiority could be made then colonialism itself would collapse. Stark was not prepared to pave that road because no one would travel on it. In this chapter it will be shown that Stark's conclusion in 1934 — that Jowitt's liberal approach to African education would cause a major problem for the colonial government — was the beginning of one major problem in African education of the post-Jowitt period. That Stark was in the forefront of protecting colonial political interests by limiting the development of African education does not mean he was the only colonial official to operate under this belief. He found a reliable ally in Godfrey Huggins (who later became Lord Malvern).

Huggins Assumes Political Power

How did Huggins, prime minister from September 12, 1933 to September 6, 1953, come to share Stark's views? The circumstances that brought Huggins to power were typical of the conditions which influenced colonial political behavior. A physician who arrived in Zimbabwe in 1911, Huggins was known among his patients as a conservative and orthodox general practitioner who had no time for innovative ideas. Indeed, Huggins practiced medicine not because he wanted to make it his career but because he wanted to establish a political base. The national debate in 1923 about the referendum to determine the future of the British South African Company administration brought him into the political arena. Instead of talking to his patients about their medical problems, he talked about the political future of the country.

Often skeptical about the British Imperial Government's policy of promoting the advancement of Africans. Huggins threw his support behind Charles Coghlan,[3] a man respected for his moderate views. But Huggins's influence on the outcome of the referendum was quite minimal. When Coghlan died suddenly in 1927, he was succeeded by Howard Moffat,[4] the grandson of Robert Moffat, the missionary who had opened the first school for Africans at Inyati in 1859. Howard was born there.

At the time of Coghlan's death, Howard Moffat was deputy premier and former minister of mines. He was considered a man of integrity because of his missionary background, but was believed to detest the character of colonial politics because of the anti-African rhetoric that became a popular theme and standard political campaign strategy among white political aspirants. Political extremists, including Huggins, exploited his moderation to portray him as a weak leader who lacked the forcefulness and the leadership they believed were required during a time of great economic difficulties and political turbulence.

Recognizing an opportunity for assuming the reins of power in a political vacuum, Huggins formed the Rhodesia Reform Party, drawing his support mainly from the dissident elements of Moffat's Rhodesia Party.[5] During the election campaign of 1928, Huggins attracted national attention with his anti-African rhetoric. Such rhetoric had characterized colonial politics since Cecil John Rhodes used it to come to power in the Cape parliament in 1895. Any person who sought political power used anti-African rhetoric to climb the political ladder. It was the only viable route to national prominence, and Huggins was only being true to a colonial tradition that had paid heavy political dividends in the past.

But because Huggins was a relative newcomer to the political scene, the voters preferred to return Moffat to power. However, in 1930, when Moffat opposed the Land Apportionment Act of 1929 in favor of moderation in the government's approach to Afgrican advancement, his popularity among whites began to decline. Also, the action his government took in 1930 to protect the economy shattered by the Great Depression, and the purchase of mineral rights from the defunct British South African Company for $4 million when many thought they should have been acquired free of charge, brought sharp criticism from Huggins. Hence Huggins's image among the whites was suddenly elevated as someone to whom they could entrust their future. Unable to weather the political storm he had not caused and could not control, and with his government greatly weakened by poor public opinion, Moffat resigned on July 4, 1933, in favor of George Mitchell,[7] another moderate, in an effort to restore the confidence of whites in the government. In many ways Moffat was the Herbert Hoover of colonial Zimbabwe: He was a victim of the Great Depression and the prevailing difficult economic conditions.

Deciding that he needed a new mandate from the voters, Mitchell dissolved parliament in August 1933, less than two months after he had succeeded Moffat, and called for new elections. Huggins had the chance of a lifetime. Extreme members of the Rhodesia Party abandoned Mitchell and joined the ranks of the Rhodesia Reform Party. The election campaign was marked by a lack of clearly articulated issues, except for the continuation of anti-African rhetoric and the problem of finding ways to minimize the effects of the Depression. When the election results were known in September, Huggins had won with a slim majority. Mitchell, like his mentor Moffat, went into the cave of political oblivion. Huggins became prime minister on September 12.

But, with a slim majority in parliament, Huggins faced a new crisis he had not anticipated. The effects of the Depression were more devastating than in 1929. Transport and essential services had come to a halt. When he tried to introduce a new railways bill, there was so much opposition that Huggins not only withdrew it but also dissolved the Rhodesia Reform Party and reactivated the Rhodesia Party, hoping to restore its reputation to what it had been during the leadership of the charismatic Coghlan.

The Alliance Between Huggins and Stark: Creating Problems for African Education

While he was working on his political strategy to win the new elections, Huggins was having secret discussions with Stark about formulating an educational policy for Africans that whites would support. The reason for secrecy was that neither man wanted to subject the major features of that policy to public scrutiny while it was being developed. That Huggins used it as a major political strategy to win the elections of 1934 with a comfortable majority shows how cruel colonial politics was. What appealed to the voters[8] was what Huggins called parallel development for the two racial groups.

Huggins's underlying philosophy was that each race should be allowed to develop under its own conditions, the whites according to their Western cultural traditions and the Africans according to their tribal traditions. As Huggins and Stark saw it, the two races had nothing in common except only in a master-servant relationship. Without any political leverage through the electoral process, the Africans were at the mercy of Huggins and Stark. It was not by coincidence that the introduction of compulsory education for white students in 1935, which the whites hoped would protect them from the threat of the Africans, occurred in the same year that Stark was confirmed as director of native education. In 1938, when Stark felt secure in his position, Huggins decided that it was time to state clearly the policy of his government on the place of the Africans in society.

After consulting with Stark, Huggins spoke in parliament in a way that surprised only a few:

> The Europeans in this country can be likened to an island in a sea of black, with the artisan

> and tradesman forming the shore and the professional class the highland in the center. Is the Native to be allowed to invade the shores and gradually attack the highland? To permit this would mean that the haven of civilization would be removed from the country and the Native would revert to a barbarism worse than before.[9]

This is exactly the same position Stark had taken as inspector of schools in 1930. Huggins went on to say "While there is still time, the country must be developed between white areas and black areas to protect both the shores and the island."[10] To accomplish this objective, Huggins and Stark decided that the educational policy for Africans must be developed from the perspective of its intended objectives, which had always been the primary concern among whites. When, in 1936, the Fox Commission affirmed the main recommendations of the Tate Commission of 1929 — that "It is essential for education to help maintain from generation to generation the cultural inheritance which is the way of life of civilized man of Western origin,"[11] — the alliance between Huggins and Stark was fully established. Huggins used the election campaign of 1939 to define an educational policy consistent with his philosophy of separation of the races.

At that time, education had become a more sensitive political issue than all other national issues combined. Also, the impact of the Great Depression was no longer as traumatic as it had been in 1930. The renewed confidence in the future had increased substantially because Britain, under the arrangements made at the time of the introduction of the "responsible government" in 1924, was slowly abandoning its constitutional responsibility to protect the Africans. Huggins could not have been happier.

These were the circumstances which Huggins took into consideration when outlining the essential elements of the new educational policy of his government, in order to convince the voters that academic education for Africans would not be considered then and for the future. It was believed to be a threat to the power and influence the whites had enjoyed for so long. Both he and Stark knew that this was the kind of policy the white voters would support. In adding that good academic education was critically important for the white students, Huggins explained why saying:

> This is essential if all our children are to be given equal opportunity for progress and to keep their position of influence and power. . . . It will prevent the creation of a poor white class. Constant adjustment will take place and the result should be a system of education Rhodesian in character, and especially suited to our own requirements.[12]

There is no question that Huggins and Stark entered a political alliance that had severe implications for African education. That Huggins began to put his philosophy into practice as soon as he felt secure in 1936 shows how carefully he designed his strategy. This is evident in his introduction of a bill into the all-white parliament in 1937. Entitled The Native Registration Bill, this legislation became law after only a brief and uneventful debate. In arguing that requiring the Africans to carry pass books at all times would help reduce "offenses resulting from the impact of an uncivilized people interacting with our civilization,"[13] Huggins was suggesting that the

Africans must constantly be reminded of their presumed uncivilized position in the colonial society, and that the educational process must be such that their differences from whites were sustained, not eliminated. This is why, in the same year, he hreatened "to deport the so-called educated Natives who are complaining about what they claim to be a lack of equal educational opportunity."[14] Huggins saw Africans as inferior to whites regardless of the level of their education, and no one must attempt to change this position.

Huggins's belief that education must condition the Africans to tribal life found expression during a debate on a bill to ban Africans from becoming permanent residents of the urban areas. He rhetorically asked the members of parliament and the white community in general "whether our municipal areas should be polyglotted with a mixture of black and white or whether we should proceed with the policy of segregation envisaged in the Land Apportionment Act and keep our towns as white as possible? The Native is a visitor in our towns for the sole purpose of serving the whites."[15] This clearly shows that the educational policy pursued by Huggins and Stark was a major problem that Africans faced in their struggle for advancement.

That this problem was compounded by Stark's lack of knowledge of the Africans' real educational needs is evident in what he failed to do. He willingly surrendered to the racist political game that Huggins was playing with so much success. He allowed creation the all-white Native Affairs Department, which Huggins charged with the responsibility of monitoring the purported development of the Africans but which, in real practice, retarded it. He compromised sound educational principles in order to please Huggins and thus ensure his own career. The inevitable outcome was that the education of Africans was at the mercy of colonial politicians who created problems to ensure their own political survival.

That the Huggins-Stark alliance was the major problem African education encountered is evident in more ways than the implementation of a policy which reduced the Africans to the status of cheap laborers and confined them to tribal life. Not only did Huggins and Stark deny the Africans equal opportunity for academic education at the primary level, but they were totally opposed to secondary education. In 1949, for example, when the Methodist Church applied for government permission to start a secondary school for Africans at Old Mutare, Charles S. Davies, senior inspector in the province, acting on Stark's instructions, furnished the following reasons why the school should not be opened:

> This will require two classrooms and necessary boarding accommodation for the 30 students. In addition, there is the major question of staff. Secondary teaching is very different from primary teaching. It is a very capable person who can teach English, Latin, Physics, Chemistry, Mathematics, and Biology at the secondary level.[16]

Davies's attitude was typical among colonial officials: that teaching academic courses to African students was made much harder by their inferior intellectual endowments. Because both Huggins and Stark failed to see the need to formulate an effective policy to ensure good secondary academic education for the Africans, they also failed to see the importance of training teachers to meet the needs at that level.

Nonetheless, in 1939, the Christian Conference managed to prevail upon the government to raise the entrance qualifications for teacher training courses to Standard VI. Even then the numbers of secondary teachers were so small that their impact on African education was minimal. The following table shows the number of African students in post-primary teacher training schools for the period 1940-1950:

Year	Number of Training Schools	Number of Students		
		Male	Female	Total
1940	12	126	22	148
1945	13	155	61	216
1950	18	263	71	334

Source: The Report of the Kerr Commission, 1951.

Huggins and Stark failed to realize that good academic education for Africans was a right that must be considered in relation to the educational needs of both the individual learner and the interests of the country as a whole and that is was utterly wrong to pursue a policy which divided the educational process into categories determined by the racial origins of recipients. In denying Africans equal educational opportunity, Huggins and Stark created a set of conditions that eventually forced the colonial government to pay the ultimate price. If Huggins and Stark had appreciated this truth, the educational process would have offered both racial groups an opportunity to build bridges of human understanding and communication from which Huggins and Stark could have engaged in a collective effort to solve the problems they had created.

Problems of African Education in Perspective: The End of the Partnership Between Horse and Rider

When Stark argued in 1934 that the Africans must work out their own educational salvation, he recognized the extent of the problems they faced in their efforts to secure good education, but did little to help solve them. There is no doubt that the problems of African education centered on t the curriculum. In 1936 Stark recognized this when he wrote in his annual report, "The curriculum of the training school is a very crowded one."[17] It entailed a number of industrial courses — carpentry, building, agriculture,leather work, and so on — that, because they were not directly related, were incoherent and inconsistent with the Africans' real educational needs. Stark preferred to ignore the fact that this was the result of his own action calculated to eliminate academic courses.

The absence of academic education and the opening of the first secondary school (St. Augustine's School at Penhalonga) in 1939, attracted the attention of influential people in Britain and in Zimbabwe. The argument that Huggins and Stark had used for denying Africans equal educational opportunity, that they were less gifted intellectually, was no longer valid by 1945. The debate that had started in the nineteenth century with the hypothesis that Africans possessed little or no intellectual capacity had to give way to a new hypothesis, that the policy of the colonial government itself was the major problem in African education.

The leadership quality that Aaron Jacha, John Dube, Clement Kadalie, and Thompson Samkange showed in the rise of African consciousness forced a change in the way whites perceived the educational development of Africans. As early as 1924, Frederick Clark, professor of education at the University of Cape Town, argued in an essay that in denying Africans an equal educational opportunity, colonial society was denying itself an opportunity for advancement: ''Our attempt to divide the indivisible will cost us dearly. No system of education that is divided into arbitrary sections by race can provide answers to national problems. The sooner we come to regard the system of education as one organic national unity, the better.''[18] Clark was, in effect, suggesting that the colonial government was attempting to perpetuate inequality in the educational process at the peril of national development.

In concluding that the educational advancement of Africans was crucial to the development of the country, the Barnes Commission of 1929 recommended that a better education than practical training be introduced into the curriculum.[19] It was clear that the Barnes Commission supported Clark's conclusion: ''The emergence of national leaders of marked ability among Natives in organization and statesmanship, the important role they have played in the development of the country and the rise of self-consciousness leave no room for doubt regarding the educability of the Africans.''[20]

Thus, the Barnes Commission also supported Jowitt's belief in the educability of Africans. Jowitt had said in 1928, ''We can hardly educate the Native without retaining our belief in his educability.''[21] All this goes to prove that by 1945 Huggins and Stark knew they could no longer justify their denial of equal educational opportunity to Africans on the myth and assumption that they were intellectually inferior. They were under pressure to provide good academic education on equal basis with whites at the primary and secondary levels and also at the post-secondary level. As these events progressed, Huggins and Stark became defensive, trying hard to preserve the structure of an educational system that was being severely criticized as shortsighted and designed to serve the interests of whites at a time when such an approach was being questioned. Both knew that their options were steadily diminishing.

One must put this development into the context of critically important developments taking place at the time. Unwilling to leave the critical question of African educational advancement to colonial officials, in 1943 the British government named a high-level commission of inquiry under the chairmanship of A. C. Asquith, a judge of the British Supreme Court, to study the educational situation in the African colonies and to make recommendations. Needless to say, Huggins and Stark were not interested in such a commission. Fully aware of the implications of its task, the Asquith Commission lived up to expectations by trying to establish an impressive list of principles that would lead to the development of institutions of higher learning in all of British colonial Africa.

In an effort to bring about a change of thinking among colonial officials concerning the role of education, especially for the colonized masses, in national development, the Asquith Commission concluded that the starting point in seeking to fulfill this fundamental objective was a definition of an institution of higher learning, which it saw as a place of training for men and women that would equip them with the skills necessary for effective national service. This definition was clearly incompatible with the narrow definition that Huggins and Stark had formulated in 1936.

In emphasizing that "It is not enough that a professional man should attain competence in his own subject both in the pursuit of his profession, and as a member of society,"[22] the Asquith Commission appeared to direct its attack toward the reluctance of the Huggins administration to move along the lines of development that it outlined. In declining to consider this possibility, Huggins and Stark stood condemned by public opinion, especially among the Africans. For Huggins and Stark the Asquith Commission was a conspiracy, a stab in the back by their political power base. To other members of the community, they had become the villains of a system that had to go because it had become the problem.

Among the principles the Asquith Commission considered essential for institutions of higher learning was the view that both Huggins and Stark rejected: that "Universities should be open to all without distinction of wealth and without discrimination on the grounds of race, sex, and creed."[23] Because colonialism thrived on racism, Huggins and Stark found themselves faced with a dilemma: to accept the recommendation of the commission and pave way for the introduction of equal educational opportunity, and thus face the prospect of the collapse of the colonial system or to reject it and face widespread criticism and threats from rising African nationalism. That they decided to reject the recommendation suggests how strongly both felt. In doing so, they opened an entirely new chapter in the relationship between the two races. They also allowed the country to see that the educational policy they pursued was the major problem facing African education.

Huggins and Stark rejected the main recommendation of the Asquith Commission, that racial discrimination had no place in the educational process because they believed it was an assault on their philosophy of relegating the education of the Africans to tribal settings. For the first time since the whites had came into contact with Africans, Huggins and Stark faced a problem that no previous colonial officials had faced: the demand for racial equality as a condition of social justice and national advancement. This critical situation was heightened by the conference of African leaders held in London at the conclusion of the war, signaling the rise of African nationalism was to affect racial relations and political development in colonial Africa in a profound way. If they had operated under normal logic, Huggins and Stark would have started packing, for the writing was clearly on the wall of their political castle. Unfortunately, they chose to face the storming of that castle rather than abandon it in order to save their political lives.

While they did not address the question of African nationalism directly, the members of the Asquith Commission must have been conscious of the political problems their report was likely to cause the colonial government: "The main consideration in our minds is not only to fulfill our moral obligation, but it is also to lead to the exercise of self-government by the colonized people."[24] Huggins and Stark knew they had to accept the inevitable or face serious political problems. The conclusion of the Asquith Commission that racial discrimination could no longer be used to deny Africans equal educational opportunity was the main reason why the Central African Council, a private organization whose members were established men of considerable influence in colonial politics in both Zimbabwe and Britain, named a new commission in September 1952 to examine the feasibility of establishing a non racial college along the lines recommended by the Asquith Commission. Its chairman was Alexander Carr-Saunders the director of the London School of Economics.

When the Carr-Saunders Commission recommended that "The proposed university should offer the best means of counteracting the influence of racial difference and sectional rivalries which impede the formation of political institutions on national basis,"[25] Huggins felt that the battle lines between the forces of white supremacy and colonial domination, which he and Stark represented, and those of racial equality, which the commission represented, had been drawn and that the storming of their political castle was about to begin. The circumstances surrounding the naming of the Carr-Saunders Commission were as important as its findings and recommendations. In 1949, wishing to launch an attack on the Huggins-Stark philosophy, and knowing that it represented a highly negative colonial attitude toward the educational development of Africans, the Central African Council named Harold Cartmel-Robinson chairman of a committee to consider the need for facilities for higher education for Africans in accordance with the guidelines set out by the Asquith Commission.

In November 1950, the Cartmel-Robinson Committee made two recommendations that cut across the Huggins-Stark philosophy. The first was that such facilities should be established to enable Africans to receive higher education on the basis of total equality with whites.[26] The second was that a new commission should be named to work out the details of how to provide these facilities. The second recommendation is what led the Central African Council to name the Carr-Saunders Commission.

Not only did the Carr-Saunders Commission strongly recommend the establishment of facilities for college education for Africans on a non racial basis, it also suggested how the colonial government could set aside funds, recommending "scholarships for higher education, either from their own resources or by seeking an additional allocation from the Colonial Development and Welfare Fund."[27] Huggins and Stark knew that the days of using rhetoric to express their opposition to the educational development of Africans were over. When the multi racial University College of Rhodesia and Nyasaland finally opened its doors in March 1956, Huggins and Stark were out of the picture. They could not stand to see the dismantling of a philosophy that had taken them two decades to implement.

Worse still, Huggins and Stark appeared to be totally unaware that the strategy of these commissions, beginning with the Asquith Commission, to discredit their philosophy on the education of Africans was paying off. The basis of their argument against providing Africans a good academic education had been destroyed. The influential people began to convince the ordinary citizens that there was no way the future of whites could be ensured without ensuring that of Africans through educational development, and that there was no way higher education could become a reality without making secondary education a reality. What had been hurting the Africans was that they were becoming increasingly isolated from the mainstream of social thought in the country.

Thus, Huggins and Stark were caught in a political net of their own making. This spelled the end of their political careers the "dual alliance" that had withstood severe criticism for 20 years. Their refusal to support the Cartmel-Robinson Committee and the Carr-Saunders Commission, and to abide by their recommendations, led to a loss of the power they had ruthlessly exercised over two decades. Finding themselves in a no-win situation, Huggins and Stark attempted to design a new strategy in an effort to retain their diminishing political power. The contradictory positions they took on the question of race and education were typical of the behavior of the colonial officials. On December 21, 1950, responding to a question following a political campaign speech, Huggins stated: "We can only build this country as partners. At the present stage of development of the backward people,it is not easy for observers to realize that we believe in a policy of racial partnership, the kind that exists between the horse and the rider."[28]

To understand Huggins's attitude, one must remember what Stark had said in 1930: that it was up to the Africans to promote their own development. The irony of what Huggins said was not only that he wanted to see the Africans become a good horse, in his definition of partnership, but also that they must train themselves to be one. Where would such a policy lead the country? For the next two years there was a wave of criticism against Huggins. There were calls for his apology and for his resignation. During that time government operations came to a halt as political dissension within the ranks of the colonial hierarchy resulted in total disarray. Wherever Huggins went, Africans received him with demonstrations and jeers. For several months nothing was heard of Stark. There was a major crisis within the "dual alliance" itself.

Faced with the reality that the end was near, Huggins came out swinging as he vigorously defended his policy, saying in 1952:

> You can call me an Imperialist of the old school. I detest the attitude of the people who condemn imperialism. True imperialism entails paternalism. It would be outrageous to give the Native a so-called political partnership and equal educational opportunity when he is likely to ruin himself as a result.[29]

On September 6, 1953, Huggins resigned to become prime minister of the ill-fated Federation of Rhodesia and Nyasaland. The lack of confidence of the people forced him to resign after only three years. This action set the stage for the Africans to struggle for a majority government. In 1954 Stark resigned for reasons of poor health. The partnership that had been forced to exist between the horse and the rider had come to an end. Now the Africans wanted to be the rider.

Summary and Conclusion

In this chapter we have discussed how the educational policies that Huggins and Stark formulated for Africans became a major problem. From 1934 to 1945, they enjoyed an unprecedented popularity among the whites because they successfully used the traditional colonial anti-African political rhetoric to a maximum political advantage. With no significant voice in how their education was being run, the Africans were at their mercy. The release of the Asquith Report in 1945, the Cartmel-Robinson Report in 1950, and the Carr-Saunders Report in 1953 proved to be their undoing. How does one explain their demise? By adhering to the traditional colonial attitude toward Africans, by refusing to see the need to adjust to new conditions, by pretending that the colonial system would last at least a thousand years as Cecil Rhodes predicted at the height of his power in 1895, and by disregarding the opinion of influential individuals in both Britain and Zimbabwe, Huggins and Stark put themselves into a corner from which they could not escape.

The problems their educational policies created for Africans turned out to be the weapon with which they inflicted mortal political wounds on themselves. The kind of damage they had worked so hard to prevent for the whites was becoming a reality before their eyes. The sad thing was that they knew they could do nothing about it. They had become so removed from reality that it was impossible for them to find a face-saving solution. Huggins and Stark had become the victims of their own philosophy and strategy. Both the Africans and the white moderates believed that with the end of the policy of "partnership between the horse and the rider," a genuine effort must now be made to improve the education of Africans in order to promote national development. The problems they had created for African education over a period of 20 years had inflicted severe damage that could not be repaired completely until the end of the colonial system. In Chapter 6 we will discuss how the alliance between Huggins and Stark affected church-state involvement in African education in an effort to revive the elements of institutional cooperation, which had come into being in the nineteenth century but which they found hard to apply to the conditions of the mid-twentieth century.

Notes

1. George Stark, The Annual Report of the Director of Native Education, 1934, p. 1.
2. Harold Jowitt, The Annual Report of the Director of Native Education, 1929, p. 7.
3. Premier from October 1, 1923, to September 1, 1927.
4. Prime Minister from September 2, 1927, to July 4, 1933.
5. The influence of this historical precedence on future developments cannot be ignored. In 1962, when Huggins's United Federal Party was weakened by circumstances it could not control, Ian Smith and Winston Field broke away to form the Rhodesia Front Party and drew their support from the dissident elements of the UFP, setting in motion events that led to a devastating civil war beginning in April 1966 and ending with the independence of Zimbabwe in April 1980.
6. This highly racially discriminatory law set aside 70 percent of the land for exclusive occupation by whites, and the remaining 30 percent, called native reserves, for exclusive occupation by Africans. The law remained in force until it was superseded by the Land Tenure Act of 1969, which was even more discriminatory.
7. Prime minister of colonial Zimbabwe from July 5, 1933, to September 11, 1933. Mitchell served the shortest tenure of any political leader in the history of colonial Zimbabwe.
8. At the time the Africans did not have the vote. The Bantu Voters Association concerned itself only with local township matters. The Africans were allowed to claim the right to vote in national elections under the Constitution of 1961. Even then, only about 5 percent met the qualifications to vote.
9. Godfrey Huggins, during a debate in parliament, in Southern Rhodesia, Legislative Debates, 1938, p. 211.
10. Ibid., p. 212
11. The Report of the Commission of Inquiry into Education, Frank Tate, Chairman, Ref.127/L4604, 1929, p. 2. In the Zimbabwe National Archives.
12. Godfrey Huggins,''Education Policy in Southern Rhodesia: Notes on Certain Features, 1939. In the Zimbabwe National Archives.
13. Godfrey Huggins, during a debate in the legislature, in Southern Rhodesia: Legislative Debates, April 2, 1937, p. 117
14. Ibid., p. 118
15. Ibid., p. 119
16. C. S. Davies, senior Inspector of Schools in Mutare, in a letter dated September 8, 1949, addressed to the superintendent of instruction at Old Mutare Methodist Center. By courtesy of the Old Mutare Methodist Archives.
17. George Stark, The Annual Report of the Director of Native Education, 1936, p. 17.
18. Frederick Clark, ''The Unity of Education,'' in The Cape Times, November, 1924., p. 3
19. Commission of Inquiry into Native Education [B.H. Barnes, Chairman], 1929, p. 14.
20. Ibid., p. 16.
21. Harold Jowitt, The Annual Report of the Director of Native Education, 1928, p. 7.
22. The British Colonial Office, The Report of the Commission on Higher Education in the Colonies A. C. Asquith, Chairman: Cmd 6647. London: His Majesty's Stationery Office, May 3, 1945, p. 12.
23. Ibid., p. 13
24. Ibid., p. 15.
25. The Central African Council, The Report of the Commission of Inquiry on Higher Education for Africans in Central Africa [Alexander Carr-Saunders, Chairman], 1953, p. 19.
26. Central African Council, The Report of the Commission of Inquiry into the Feasibility of Establishing Facilities for Higher Education for Africans in Central Africa [Harold Cartmel-Robinson, Chairman], 1950, p. 7.
27. The Carr-Saunders Report, p. 59.
28. Godfrey Huggins, ''Partnership in Building a Country,'' a political campaign speech, December 21, 1950. In the Zimbabwe National Archives.
29. Godfrey Huggins, a political campaign speech, 1952.

6
Stark's Role in Church-State Involvement in African Education: The Search for a New Institutional Partnership

Racial discrimination is a major obstacle to successful African education. — The Kerr Commission, 1951

The more primitive the Africans, the easier the problem, both to educate and to control. — Godfrey Huggins, 1954

The Change of White Attitude Toward Africans

One important effect of the recommendations of the Asquith Commission, the Cartmel-Robinson Committee, and the Carr-Saunders Commission was a change of white attitude in a way no one could have predicted. Before 1945, colonial politicians paved their way to the top of the political ladder by espousing anti-African political views. Any aspiring colonial politician who advocated moderation was rejected by the voters. Expressing racial views against the Africans had always yielded heavy political dividends since Cecil Rhodes adopted this strategy in 1895. Every colonial politician who attempted to lay a claim to being Rhodes's successor used extreme anti-African rhetoric. That is how Huggins remained in office for 20 years.

Beginning with the release of the Asquith Report, and much to the dismay of Huggins and Stark, aspiring politicians now found it necessary to pave their way to national prominence by espousing ideas favorable to Africans. It became fashionable for politicians to argue that they were men of vision and goodwill who demanded that the future of Africans be safeguarded because it was right for whites to do so. It remained to be seen whether this claimed change of attitude was real. However, overnight, Huggins and Stark were faced with the reality of a new situation that placed them in an untenable political position. Because they refused to accept, at least in principle, the change of attitude that many of their compatriots were embracing as an imperative of the times, Huggins and Stark became increasingly isolated.

Not only did they become embarrassed by their efforts to retain the traditional negative colonial attitude toward Africans, but they also became social misfits and removed from a mainstream of the social environment that favored a more accommodating approach to the question of race. The underlying principle central to this apparent change of attitude among whites seems to have been the thinking that the educational advancement of Africans was the best way to ensure their socioeconomic security. This was also considered to be the best way of ensuring the security of whites and while it was still possible, the whites must help Africans to realize that advancement. Thus, the Asquith Commission, the Cartmel — Robinson Committee, and the Carr — Saunders Commission must be given the credit for bringing about a much needed change of attitude among whites.

That whites themselves felt it was important to criticize the government's educational policy helps to explain the extent of the change that was taking place within colonial society. For example, on February 9, 1946, the Methodist Church called for new church-state initiative to improve African education. In arguing, "We affirm that education is the dual responsibility of both the Church and the State, each having its own sphere of duty,"[1] the Methodist Church was, in effect, suggesting that the colonial government reevaluate its policy toward the education of Africans in light of the change in thinking that was taking place. But while it was sincere in making this suggestion, was the Methodist Church realistic in expecting Huggins and Stark to accept ideas moving toward church — state involvement in the conduct of African education?

Circumstances Surrounding the Naming of the Kerr Commission

Four months after the Methodist Church made its call, Garfield Todd,[2] a senior member of Huggins's administration, surprised the country and angered Huggins by publicly criticizing the educational policy of a government of which he was a senior member. In characterizing a policy that allocated an expenditure of $0.40 per African student and $20.00 per white student[3] as a national disgrace, Todd underscored the urgent need to redesign educational policy so that it would result in equal opportunity for the students of both races.

A disturbing aspect of the post - Asquith claim of change of attitude among whites is that while whites recognized the need to do something dramatic in the conduct of African education, none called for racial integration in both society and the schools. They seemed to neglect the fact that as long as the school system remained segregated by race, it was futile to talk of equal educational opportunity for all students. Todd and many other liberals fell victim to this shortcoming. Calling for an end to racial discrimination in all its forms was a risk that many colonial politicians did not want to take.

A former missionary from New Zealand, Todd had been principal of Dadaya School for Africans for some years before he entered active politics in 1946. The problems the African students encountered due to inadequate colonial policy was the main reason he decided to enter politics. He believed he could use his missionary background and awareness of the problems to make a difference. When he recognized Huggins's unwillingness to move toward providing equal educational opportunity to all students, Todd decided to launch a national campaign to force the issue. Speaking before the Bulawayo National Affairs Association in February 1947, Todd called for a commission of inquiry into African education and warned Huggins about the consequences of continuing his existing policy:

> The Africans are aware that educated people can be governed, but they cannot be enslaved forever. They are no longer willing to be controlled in the manner in which they have been controlled in the past. There is a spirit of urgency. Guide it, give it assistance, and there will develop a people who will be a credit to this country. Disregard that spirit of urgency or hinder or cripple it in any way, an adverse effect will result racially.[4]

Huggins and Stark felt betrayed by a man they thought supported official policy, a typical reaction of those unwilling to adjust to new situations.

Aware that the Huggins-Stark educational policy was designed to fulfill two main objectives — to prepare Africans to function as cheap laborers and to condition them to tribal settings — Todd argued that this policy was intended to ensure colonial control of Africans and, thus, of the country. Because the education the Africans received under this policy did not produce individuals who were complete, he concluded that it had to be changed in order to prepare the Africans for full participation in a dynamic society. He asked Huggins and Stark to appoint a commission to study the situation and come up with an answer.[5]

If Huggins and Stark had reason to believe they were two supermen in the conduct of educational policy for Africans, that image had been seriously tarnished by a widespread belief among whites that their obsession with practical training had plunged the educational process into total disarray. This explains why the views Todd expressed were shared by Africans. In an editorial one week after Todd's speech, *The African Weekly* addressed this critical question:

> The African view is that since education is the complete formation of the whole man, what reason is there to classify the educational process into black education and white education? To the Africans the term "Native Education" carries with it such labels as little finances, inferior equipment, few qualified teachers. The product of this is a man ill-fitted for the economic, social, and political life in the colony. We favor a system of education based on total equality and which shapes all people so that they come into a world which gives them a hope for the future, not despair and bitterness, as the Africans are now experiencing.[6]

Like Todd and the Methodist Church, *The African Weekly* concluded by calling for a commission of inquiry into African education with the purpose of removing all inequalities that handicapped the education of Africans and of enabling them to adjust to new political and socioeconomic conditions.

The wave of continuing criticism against the Huggins-Stark educational policy aroused the indignation of many individuals who supported Todd's call for a commission of inquiry. This was the line of thinking of Reverend Kennedy Grant, a leading priest in the Anglican Church, when he argued in September 1947:

> The aim of education should be to train our pupils in the art of living together. Education is a continuous process of developing a personality which is essential to human relationship. The foundations of all good living are built on man's relationship with his own fellow man.[7]

In urging Huggins and Stark to name a commission to study ways of ending educational inequality, Reverend Grant was joining the chorus warning them of the consequence of attempting to sustain the existing educational policy: a rapid deterioration in human relationships. Huggins responded by arguing that his administration had a policy of encouraging human relationships, the horse - rider style. To appreciate why there was an outcry against the educational policy pursued by Huggins and Stark, one needs to understand what African education was going through. In 1949 male certificated teachers earned an annual income of $168.00, compared with $111.98 for certificated female teachers. These were 60 percent less than salaries paid in industry. This was a major reason why, by 1950, 45 percent of all teachers resigned to take jobs elsewhere.

In 1951, only 30 percent of the teachers were certificated. In the same year 66.9 percent of the Grade I (known as Sub-standard A) pupils were able to go on to second grade.The emphasis on practical training produced less than 15 percent literacy among the Africans. In the same year, the government spent 96.5 percent of the national education budget, ($32,361,140.00) for white education and the remainder ($1,178,524.00) on African education.[8] There were fears that continuing the policy of practical training, as it was being implemented by Huggins and Stark, would lead to an illiterate population within a decade, and that this must be changed immediately.

Huggins's and Stark's Roles in the Kerr Commission

These were the facts that Huggins and Stark found hard to refute, and constituted the circumstances that forced them to name a commission of inquiry. At last they had acknowledged the serious weaknesses at the center of their policy. The public rejected their argument that there was no need for a commission of inquiry because everything was going well in African education. That they named a commission three years after Todd first raised the question shows how reluctant they were to take the risk its report was likely to pose.

In 1950, in an effort to silence the critics of their policy, fearing the implications of political indiscretion, and because every attempt to avoid it had failed, Huggins and Stark named Alexander Kerr, a conservative educator considered a leading expert on the problems of African education in South Africa, chairman of the commission. A former president of Fort Hare College for Africans near Cape Town, Kerr seemed equal to the task.

The terms of reference of the Kerr Commission were as loosely stated as those of the Graham Commission of 1911, a strategy Huggins and Stark designed so that it would return a report favorable to their policy. Their naming Kerr[9] suggests how hopeful they were that he was sympathetic to their policy. But, compelled by the sad state of African education, the Kerr Commission chose to embarrass Huggins and Stark rather than attempt to conceal the grim situation its study had revealed. After visiting 115 schools and hearing evidence from people who wanted to appear before it, the Kerr Commission submitted its report in 1951. The evidence that came before the commission led Kerr to the inevitable conclusion that Huggins and Stark were pursuing a racial philosophy and educational policies that were totally out of touch with reality. In a candid and thoroughly professional manner, the Kerr Commission concluded that the lack of adequate government policy on African education was the major problem and must be resolved immediately.[10]

There is no doubt that Huggins and Stark were displeased when the Kerr Commission put the implications of this conclusion into the perspective of historical developments, of which their own administration was an important segment:

> Events since the War have shown how profound the effects of education are, not only on individuals, but also on groups. For education creates ideas and awakens desires which, when they are ill-directed or unsatisfied, are calculated to cause frustration and discontent and even hatred towards those who have been the source of their meaningless education.[11]

The Kerr Commission wanted to be sure that Huggins and Stark understood the message it intended for them. ''Frustration,'' ''discontent,'' and ''hatred'' were quite strong terms for a high-level commission to use to describe the sorry state of African education. The commission wanted to leave no room for misunderstanding.

The report took Huggins and Stark by surprise. Never before had a commission appointed by the government felt compelled, by the weight of the evidence before it, to level such criticism. Since Huggins and Stark had assumed office, in 1933 and 1934, respectively, this was the first severe criticism of their policy to be expressed by members of the colonial establishment. If Huggins and Stark had hoped that the Kerr Commission would submit a report blindly supporting their philosophy and educational policies, that hope vanished under the preponderance of the evidence before it. This was as much a shock to them as it was to Kerr. The reality of the situation confronted the Kerr Commission and forced it to remind Huggins and Stark that they had an obligation to design an educational policy for Africans on the basis of total equality with whites. The commission knew that Huggins and Stark would fail to implement its recommendations. This was precisely what they did.

Among the findings of the Kerr Commission that Huggins and Stark found difficult to accept was evidence suggesting that equal educational opportunity for Africans was not only an essential component of racial peace but also the only realistic basis on which to build a new national identity. The commission report stated:

> An educational program can be neither formed nor carried out in a vacuum. It is very sensitive to extraneous circumstances particularly in the matter of national character. Two sets of circumstances have seriously disrupted this, and until they are stopped, will continue to disrupt, the character of African education. These are the want of adequate provisions for home and family life and the occupational color bar.[12]

It is quite clear that the Kerr Commission was rejecting Huggins's 1950 definition of partnership and Stark's philosophy of African education. In order to stress the importance of the spirit of urgency that Todd had raised during a speech to the Bulawayo National Affairs Association on February 8, 1947, the Kerr Commission quoted the testimony of one white witness who saw the concept of equal educational opportunity for Africans from a pragmatic viewpoint: ''If education is intended to exclude Africans from skilled trade, it is a sheer nonsense to talk of producing good citizens. The Africans who are denied equal educational opportunity will soon become embittered and will be anything but good citizens.''[13] This is yet another piece of evidence to suggest that attitudes among whites were changing in favor of promoting the educational development of Africans as the best way of protecting their own future. The problem was with Huggins and Stark. Believing that they were selected custodians of Rhodes's legacy, they did not want to let go of a system that he had put in place toward the end of the nineteenth century.[14]

In concluding that equal educational opportunity was necessary for building a new national identity, the Kerr Commission was warning Huggins and Stark that there would be a price to pay for adhering to an antiquated racial philosophy and educational policy. But in all their claimed liberal views, the whites failed to recognize that genuine change in African education could occur only when there was a fundamental change in the political system. Without the right to participate in the electoral process and subject the candidates to a scrutiny of their political views and national agenda, any other course of action would yield few tangible results. It was unfortunate that the Kerr Commission failed to recognize and address the intricate relatedness between the political process and the educational process. This was the fundamental structure that sustained the colonial system. To advocate change in the educational system without advocating change in the political system was like trying to clean the water in a stream polluted by industrial emissions further up-stream.

With all that it said against Huggins and Stark, the Kerr Commission appears to have leveled its most severe criticism against racial discrimination in the educational process, which, it concluded, originated from the government view that education must condition the Africans to a tribal environment. Rejecting this view, the commission expressed its belief in the capability of Africans to contribute to national development through equal educational opportunity: ''We hold the unbound confidence in the African in order to mold his character and educate him properly. Racial discrimination therefore becomes a major obstacle to successful African education.''[15] It was evident that this was an indictment of Huggins and Stark.

Another finding of the Kerr Commission that did not set well with Huggins and Stark was that it produced figures to substantiate the accuracy of its conclusion that ''The most disconcerting feature of the system is the short school life of the African child,''[16] and that this was a result of the policy Huggins and Stark had pursued. Following are the figures the Kerr Commission cited for the school year 1950-1951:

Class	Enrollment	% of Enrollment in previous Class
Sub-standard A	80,118	—
Sub-standard B	53,592	66.9
Standard I	38,113	71.1
Standard II	25,366	66.6
Standard III	16,742	66.0
Standard IV	8,942	53.4
Standard V	5,386	60.2
Standard VI	3,000	55.7

It is evident that the Kerr Commission recognized the seriousness of this situation when it discussed its harmful effects: ''Whatever small value they may have for the future life of the child, two years of school life will not ensure the retention of any degree of literacy, even in the vernacular.''[17] Another disturbing truth that the above figures reveal is that slightly more than half of all students reached Standard VI, the last year of primary schooling. No wonder Huggins and Stark did not want to name another commission to investigate the conduct of African education: They knew it would reveal a sad picture.

Recommendations of the Kerr Commission: The Nature of Church-State Partnership

The evidence against Huggins and Stark was so overwhelming that they did not try to refute it or to defend their policy. In a situation where democracy existed, this would have forced both men to resign or would have caused the collapse of the government. There was absolutely nothing to show what their policy had accomplished in two decades except an increase in the number of unskilled African workers. The employers seem to have concluded that they really wanted to see something else in African education besides emphasis on practical training. The question that was central to the Kerr Commission was whether Huggins and Stark could withstand the political backlash that was certain to follow its report.

In order to cushion the impact of the criticism of the educational policy that Huggins and Stark pursued, the Kerr Commission tried to find something positive to say. But in doing so, it based its recommendations on its findings, whether or not it thought they would be implemented. Reminding Huggins and Stark that they had introduced free compulsory education for white students in 1935, and recognizing the brevity of the school life of African students, the Kerr Commission recommended that compulsory free education be provided to urban African students as the first phase of introducing free compulsory education throughout the country on the basis of total equality with whites. Again the commission did not suggest how this could be accomplished.

Of the 140 recommendations the Kerr Commission made, none was more important than its opinion that African education was so bad that the partnership between church and state was needed to begin the enormous task of salvaging it. But in putting forth this suggestion, the commission warned Huggins not to attempt to practice the kind of partnership he had defined in 1950.

The idea of partnership had seemed to have some appeal for the missionaries since the Waddilove Manifesto had raised it in February 1946. But Huggins was too deeply rooted in colonial thinking to understand the essential elements of the Kerr Commission's definition or the substance of its recommendations.

The Kerr Commission's emphasis on the importance for Huggins and Stark to appoint a research officer who had an expert knowledge of African sociology[18] suggests that they needed professional help in implementing these recommendations and in improving the structure of African education. An expert in African sociology would serve as a liaison between the Africans and Huggins and Stark, thereby providing better communication and reducing the likelihood of failure in the educational programs. Again, this was hard for both to accept because they thought educational decisions could be made only from a political perspective.

Reduced to its simplest form, the formula for the partnership between church and state meant observance of two basic elements. The first was that Huggins and Stark had to recognize that their educational policies constituted a major problem for the Africans, and that this problem was far too serious to be resolved through political rhetoric. They needed to understand the fundamental need to change it entirely. This meant that they had to eliminate the rigidity with which they had previously approached African education. The church must accept the authority of the government to formulate policies after consultation with its representatives. The second element in the partnership between church and state required that Huggins and Stark reverse the policies they had put in place over two decades. This was the most difficult problem they faced in addressing the recommendations of the Kerr Commission.

For the Kerr Commission to recommend that a better system of communication be initiated to improve the partnership between Huggins and Stark and the church was to ask them to recognize that a new policy had to be designed in order to make a new institutional cooperation possible. As the Kerr Commission saw things, the partnership between the government and the church in the conduct of African education would ensure mutual respect. Would Huggins and Stark see things from this angle? One must ask the obvious question: Did the recommendation of institutional partnership different from the kind Huggins defined in 1950 lead to the improvement of African education? The answer lies in the administrative structure it recommended:

> For the supervision of the 2,244 Native schools, the appointment and dismissal of teachers, the payment of subsidies and salaries in a budget totaling $14 million annually, the regulation of courses, and the general control of all matters pertaining to the education of 238,000 Africans, the government must depend upon several types of agencies, including the Church.[19]

This suggests that the techniques of implementing the institutional partnership were not as clear-cut as some might have thought. The specific responsibilities that each side was expected to fulfill to make it work were not spelled out. How could the Kerr Commission leave it to Huggins and Stark to interpret what it appeared to be saying?

One must understand the importance of two aspects the Kerr Commission did not discuss directly but that had a profound effect on the character of the institutional partnership its members had in mind. The first was that by 1951, the Africans were becoming increasingly restless about how the missionaries and the Huggins administration were running their education. With the rising influence of African nationalism, that institutional partnership was facing a crisis. The church emphasized the importance of religion and moral values, while Huggins and Stark were still emphasizing the importance of practical training and manual labor.[20] Until the Kerr Commission raised the problem posed by this contradictory strategy, Huggins and Stark had no intention of initiating changes to improve African education.

The second important aspect was that in its recommendation to continue some form of industrial training, the Kerr Commission does not appear to have considered the fact that the school population was getting younger. Hence, the character of the school population was changing rapidly. Since 1949 there had been a substantial decrease in the average age, from eight to six and half for beginning Sub-standard A; only 5 percent of these children would reach Standard III. This in turn meant that children were expected to undertake practical training at the average age of fifteen, the age at which they might complete Standard VI. How could the Kerr Commission or Huggins and Stark expect these children to make a viable contribution to the national economy without reintroducing elements of child labor?

Huggins and Stark used parts of the Kerr Report favorable to their policies to maneuver their way out of a politically explosive situation. Todd and his supporters were openly calling for both men to resign. Some whites were wondering what would happen in the near future. In 1952, instead of seeking ways to solve the problems the Kerr Commission had identified, Huggins began to play a new political game by working toward the establishment of the ill-fated Federation of Rhodesia and Nyasaland. He apparently had decided that the process of implementing the partnership along the lines the Kerr Commission had recommended was too complex.

Because less than 5 percent of Africans could meet the qualifications to vote, Huggins campaigned vigorously to convince the skeptical British government that such a federation would be in a better position to serve the interests of Africans in the three colonies (Southern Rhodesia, Northern Rhodesia, and Nyasaland were all colonies of Great Britain) than in separate ones. Thus, he made Kerr's definition of partnership into his own redefinition of partnership between his administration and the Africans. But, because the British government did not have total confidence in him, it agreed to the union of the three colonies only on a conditional basis. When evidence began to mount that the leadership was not living up to its commitment, Britain dissolved the federation in 1963, setting in motion events that led to a major national crisis.

During the three years that he served as the prime minister of the ill-fated federation (1953-1956), Huggins's attitude toward Africans hardened as he used the Kerr Report to remind them that they were not equal to whites. Speaking in August 1954, a year after he had assumed his responsibilities as prime minister of the Federation, Huggins did not hesitate to reassert the claim that he had used to bring himself to power in 1933. Arguing that the recommendations of the Kerr Commission had no bearing on his policy, Huggins said:

> It is true that the more primitive the Africans, the easier the problem, both to educate and to control. You can deal with basic matters without having to consider complications which are eventually caused when primitive man becomes, to a certain point, sophisticated thorough whatever form of education he receives.[21]

Clearly Huggins wanted Africans to understand two things. The first thing was that instead of directing their efforts toward gaining equal educational opportunity, they would be wiser if they tried to acquire the essentials of Western culture. In his view, equal educational opportunity was impossible as long as Africans retained the basic components of their culture. But what is more disturbing about the views Huggins expressed is that he failed to understand that in the African context, culture could not be separated from race; yet race, not culture, was the major criterion he used to determine the applicability of the concept of opportunity in colonial society.

The second thing was that Huggins saw institutional partnership as a means of strengthening the role of the church and weakening his own power. Thus, he decided that he did not want to implement any of the recommendations the Kerr Commission had made. The work that had gone into producing it was all for naught. However, the Africans took it upon themselves to use its recommendations to launch a campaign to restore their rights. When Huggins chose to resign rather than to face the problems he had created over 20 years, he was succeeded on September 7, 1953, by Garfield Todd. Todd found the task of rebuilding African education so enormous that he mobilized all resources to initiate the desired change. When Todd appointed himself minister of African education to ensure that his policy would be carried out as he ordered, Stark felt that he was being pushed out. When Stark resigned in 1954, both Todd and the country were pleased that at last the alliance of two men whose political fortunes were intertwined, had been removed from the scene. But in all that he tried to do, Todd was seriously handicapped by the immensity of a problem that had festered over the years.

When, in 1952, Stark tried to discredit the Kerr Commission by saying that implementing its recommendations would require $2 million that was not there,[22] he was venting his frustration over a situation that was forcing his career to an end. Ironically with all the power that they thought they had, Huggins and Stark became the ultimate victims of a system they put in place to preserve their positions. The colonial condition of which they were a part had no more mercy for them than for its intended victims, the Africans.

Summary and Conclusion

The discussion in this chapter leads to some interesting observations. If one were to determine the success or failure of the Kerr Commission by the strength of its criticism of the policies Huggins and Stark pursued, one might be led to the conclusion that it was a success. But if one were to make that determination by what it said about the Africans, then one would be led to the conclusion that it was a failure. The reason for this conclusion is that in expressing the views it did, the Kerr Commission appears to show some support for Huggins and Stark at a time when there was an overwhelmingly negative reaction to their policies.

Even in their helplessness, the Africans managed to arouse popular sentiment against a colonial government that behaved in a manner intended to serve its own political interests. The Kerr Commission knew that Huggins and Stark had inflicted great damage that could not be undone as long as they remained in office, yet it failed to call for the end of their administration. This suggests that the commission lacked the knowledge or the sensitivity needed to make a real impact on the search for solutions to a serious national problem. By failing to respond affirmatively to the demand of such people as Garfield Todd, Kennedy Grant, and Robert Tredgold for a fundamental change in the political structure so that it met the needs of all people, the Kerr Commission let down those moderate whites who had expressed faith in the Africans.

Of the 140 recommendations of the Kerr Commission, none received more attention than the one dealing with the causes of the absence of dialogue between Huggins and Stark and the Africans. This demonstrates the two men's unwillingness and their uncompromising belief in the inferiority of Africans. This is why they rejected the recommendation that: "a consultative council made up of representatives of the African teachers, parents, missionary bodies, and government officials be formed to define relationship between the government and the people."[23] If Huggins and Stark had accepted this recommendation, an environment would have been created to serve as a forum for the search for solutions to the many national problems that could not be resolved in any other way. The influence of this colonial behavior on the Rhodesia Front government of 1962 was that, like Huggins, its leaders refused to engage in dialogue with the Africans. The net result was that a bitter civil war broke out in 1966 and ended only with the collapse of the colonial government in 1979.

In addition to the contradictions of its report, the nature of the conclusions and recommendations of the Kerr Commission did not address the critically important issue of equality in society. Rather, they discussed the importance of family life. By failing to discuss political representation in its broad context, such as the introduction of a mechanism to ensure political accountability and the right to vote, the Kerr Commission was offering subtle support to Huggins and Stark at a time when many were calling for their resignation.

Therefore, the role that Huggins and Stark played in naming the Kerr Commission was the same role, in reverse, that the Kerr Commission played in their decision not to implement its recommendation. The church-state partnership the Kerr Commission recommended as a starting point in an effort to improve African education did not come into being because Huggins and Stark saw it as an attempt to undercut their power base.

Chapter 7 will discuss how the Huggins-Stark alliance was part of the crisis that African education experienced. It will also examine a crisis situation in Mangwende Native Reserve as a case study in conflict between the government and Africans over educational policy.

Notes

1. The Methodist Church, The Waddilove Manifesto: The Education Policy of the Methodist Church, February 8-9, 1946.

2. Prime Minister from September 7, 1953, to February 16, 1958.

3. Garfield Todd, ''A Plea for Better Education for Africans,'' in The African Weekly, Vol. 3, No. 2, June 12, 1946.

4. Garfield Todd, ''African Education in Southern Rhodesia: The Need for a Commission of Inquiry,'' address to the Bulawayo National Affairs Association, February 18, 1947. In the Zimbabwe National Archives.

5. Ibid.

6. The African Weekly Vol. 3, No. 38, February 26, 1947.

7. Reverend. Kennedy Grant, ''Teach the Children the Art of Living Together,'' an address to the Conference of African Teachers, September 10, 1947. In the Zimbabwe National Archives.

8. The Report of the Kerr Commission, 1951, p. 9.

9. Kerr was the only member of the Carr-Saunders Commission to submit a minority report supporting the policies Huggins and Stark were pursuing. It was speculated that Kerr resigned as president of Fort Hare College because he was so conservative that he refused to consider changes for improvement. His support of the policies Stark and Huggins seems to support this conclusion.

10. The Report of the Kerr Commission, para. 42, p. 17.

11. Ibid., para 47. 7.

12. Ibid., para.47, p.8.

13. Ibid., para. 49, p. 9

14. One cannot minimize the impact of this historical precedent to the continuing saga of conflict in Zimbabwe. While the Rhodesia Front was in power (1962-1979), the vast majority of whites indicated they wanted a policy that would move rapidly to accommodate the aspirations of the Africans. But the RF itself did not see things from this perspective. In a similar manner, the problems of South Africa are compounded by the refusal of the ruling Nationalist Party to see national problems from a more realistic perspective.

15. The Report of the Kerr Commission, para. 53, p. 9.

16. Ibid., para.82, p. 14.

17. Ibid., para. 83, p. 15.

18. Ibid.., para. 59, p. 10.

19. Ibid., para. 94, p. 16.

20. Ibid., para. 156, p. 24.

21. Godfrey Huggins, ''Taking Stock of African Education,'' an address to the Southern Rhodesia Missionary Conference at Goromonzi School, August 26, 1954. By courtesy of the Zimbabwe National Archives.

22. George Stark, The Annual Report of the Director of Native Education, 1952, p. 42.

23. The Report of the Kerr Commission, para. 341, p. 46.

7
Stark's Role in the Crisis in African Education: Case Study in Mangwende Reserve

The Council will never be happy until it has a school of its own. — H.A. Ling, Native Commission for Mangwende Native Reserve, 1953

Huggins and Stark Caught in the Middle

This study has concluded that the action of the Central African Council in naming the Cartmel-Robinson Committee in 1949 and the Carr-Saunders Commission in 1952 produced a set of conditions that seemed to climax in the public outcry, which began with the Asquith Commission, against the deliberate colonial policy of limiting the educational opportunity for Africans. Although Huggins and Stark tried, this trend could not be stopped.

That Huggins and Stark thought that this was a temporary movement to embarrass them and to arouse a political consciousness in the Africans is evidence of their gross miscalculations. They did not know that this was the beginning of a movement that could not be reversed. Further, the rise of African nationalism, beginning with the conference of African leaders at London in 1945, was a product of a combination of events, including the war itself. In refusing to support these commissions and to abide by their findings and recommendations, Huggins and Stark created the impression that they were trying to hide something radically wrong with their educational policies for Africans. Their initial attempt to decline to name the Kerr Commission was a demonstration of their bad faith in the conduct of African education.

The ultimate evidence showing how bad things really were in African education was the tragic events unfolding throughout the country. The crisis in Mangwende Reserve, which attracted national attention, shows how Huggins and Stark were caught in the middle of a situation they had created. The appointment of a commission of inquiry[1] on October 28, 1960, to investigate this crisis revealed the extent of some serious problems that Huggins and Stark created through their policy on African education, and that they tried not to let the country know about. In this chapter we will use the crisis in Mangwende Reserve as a case study to examine these problems.

The crisis, which made national headlines in 1960, began to unfold in 1937 as a result of Huggins's law. In that year the Native Councils Act came into being. Its main provision was to allow Africans to form councils to promote their own development. In 1943, Huggins introduced an amendment to this law to allow Africans to raise money for local projects and, convinced that they would not be able to do so, encouraged them by promising a matching grant. This is why, during the debate on the amendment Huggins argued: "It is like the old days in Athens when everybody met in the market square and fixed things up. When the Natives have done that they can elect people to represent them in parliament. But this is a long way off. Why be in such a hurry?''[2] Indeed, the colonial parliament remained an exclusive white club until Britain forced a new constitution in 1961, that allowed for 15 Africans in a legislature of 60 members. Huggins and those who succeeded him were in no hurry.

The Africans' ability to respond to conditions that controlled their lives was a reality Huggins did not understand. Only in 1953 did the rhetorical question he asked during the debate on the amendment prove to be a great embarrassment. That the amendment of 1943 specified the development of education must have been based on his belief that Africans were unable to see things from such an enlightened perspective. In making the promise of matching assistance, Huggins mistakenly believed the Africans would not be able to meet this challenge. Organization, procedures, collective definition of objectives, and setting priorities were, as he saw it, simple social concepts too complex for Africans to understand, let alone apply.[3]

But only three years following the reenactment of the Native Councils Act in 1943, events would prove not only that Huggins was wrong in his assessment of the African ability to understand democracy, but also that he elected not to honor his promise of matching assistance. The sudden upsurge in Africans' interest in forming councils, and their ability to articulate clear positions on issues and to formulate programs placed Huggins and Stark in a difficult situation.

The Road to a National Crisis: The Battle of Wills

This is the background of the tragic events that began to unfold on February 26, 1946, when the Africans in Mangwende Reserve formed the Mangwende Rural Council in the Mrewa District, some 50 miles east of Harare (then Salisbury), the capital city. Huggins and Stark must have been pleased with this action because they expected nothing but chaos. This would substantiate their claim that Africans were totally unable to organize an effective structure or institution consistent with any developmental objectives. The Africans wanted to prove that this assessment of their potential was a mistake, and they did.

The minutes of the very first meeting held, on June 19, 1946, reveal that the first item on the agenda the Mangwende Rural Council's agenda was education. After a thorough examination of the facts and an exhaustive debate, it voted to ask the government to build a school in the district. The ability of the Africans to understand the issues and to engage in parliamentary debate to listen, and to use logic to argue a viewpoint surprised the native commissioner, who, in keeping with the provision of the Native Councils Act, was the chairman.

It is not by accident that the council's first action was on education. In voting to ask the government to build a school, it advanced two reasons. The first was based on the fact that, beginning in 1946, the government had opened its first primary school in an urban areas, Chitsere Primary School in Harare, and the first secondary school, Goromonzi. It was therefore logical for the Mangwende Council to conclude that having decided to build these schools at no cost to the people, the government should do the same in the rural areas, and that their area should have the first.

The council concluded that for the government to build schools free of charge for

Africans in the urban areas but not for those in the rural areas, was unfair and wrong. From the very beginning of its involvement in the saga of educational controversy, the Mangwende Council understood that the educational process itself entailed political dimensions. It therefore did not accept the government viewpoint that:

> The sudden upsurge of rural interest in education coincided with the vast influx of Africans into urban areas from the early 1940's. Consequently there was the priority claim on limited government resources to build, staff and run schools in urban areas as a social necessity to safeguard against juvenile vagrancy and delinquency.[4]

The fact that the Africans could reason logically reinforced Stark's belief that their education must be confined to tribal settings. The second reason advanced by the Council for requesting that a school be built in its district was that the church-related schools in the district imposed admission conditions the council believed were contrary to the educational interests of African students.[5]

Sadly with all their claimed ability to see things from the proper perspective, Huggins and Stark were still unable to understand that:

> The groping for new standards of behavior in a fast-changing world, the powerful urge to assert an individual identity and collective purpose led to the demand for education, not for its own sake, but as an essential tool to force an entry into a world of plenty and of boundless scope for individual ambitions.[6]

The amendment of a law they thought would evince the inferiority of the Africans proved to be a nightmare for Huggins and Stark. This was the first time since the brutal war of 1896-1897 that Africans assembled and discussed issues of great importance under colonial control, and they successfully carried out their assigned tasks. This sent shock waves through the political arm of the colonial establishment. For several weeks Huggins and Stark did not know how to respond to the request for a government school. The council's first priority of education surprised them.

After consulting Huggins and Stark, H. A. Ling, the native commissioner of Mangwende Reserve, a colonial official whose responsibility was defined by the Native Councils Act of 1943 as guiding the development of Africans and assisting them in any way possible, was faced with a problem he had not anticipated. Following the instructions of Huggins and Stark, Ling, clearly groping for a plausible reason, used a provision of the law[7] to advise the council that its request for a government school had been denied because the area had enough schools to meet the educational needs of all the students.

This denial helped to set in motion a series of developments that precipitated a national crisis which began in April 1966 with the outbreak of the war of independence.[8] The Brown Commission fully understood the context in which the Mangwende Council refused to accept this denial as a final government answer even though its members and the Africans they represented knew that Huggins and Stark did not look kindly on their educational needs. The Brown Commission stated:

> It was the immediate post-war period when there was a dramatic change in attitude of the Africans towards education. The rather apathetic prewar outlook was rapidly being transformed to a general and urgent realization that education was the essential tool for gaining a foothold in a competitive and civilized modern world.[9]

In this statement it was suggesting that the Africans were objecting to old stereo-types, and were adjusting to new conditions much faster than Huggins and Stark were willing to acknowledge. The difficulties they encountered in their struggle for advancement came from the lack of sensitivity on the part of colonial officials. It is really not surprising that for rural Africans, educational opportunity became a politically sensitive topic of discussion between them and colonial officials. Such discontent easily exploded into an unpleasant situation.

It is easy to understand how the idea of a council school had a powerful appeal to the Africans and why this issue became a cause of a major conflict between them and the colonial officials. As the Africans saw things, such a school not only would become the rallying point of their search for individuality and collective purpose, but also would become a fitting symbol for a group of progressive people seeking an identity and a foundation on which to build their future. But, as Huggins and Stark saw things, a council school built at government expense, while easy to control, in both curricular content and other educational activities, would give the Africans an important voice in how government decisions were made and programs were carried out. They concluded that this would make it difficult for the government to make decisions without submitting them to the Africans for approval. Further, building a council-controlled school at government expense would set a precedent and would have serious implications for the future by limiting government freedom to set its agenda and priorities.

Given the environment in which government policy was formulated and implemented, it was hard to find another national issue causing so much mistrust and conflict between the Huggins government and the Africans. Because neither side was prepared to compromise its position, the suspicions and fears of each side about the intention of the other created the potential for a serious conflict. To Huggins and Stark it came as a shock that the Africans were putting demands on them in a way they had never done in the past: as a right, not as a privilege. To the members of Mangwende Council and the Africans it represented, it came as a shock that Huggins and Stark declined to honor a solemn promise. Therefore the two sides had two things in common, their desire to sustain their own position and their effort to prove the other wrong. This strategy of confrontation produced the setting in which a major conflict became inevitable.

Ironically this type of social conflict was an outcome of a law Huggins and Stark believed would entail "an essential administrative approach which might save the rural African society from utter disintegration,"[10] but that the Africans thought was designed to tailor their aspirations to the garment of a grand colonial design. Who was to blame for this tragic breakdown in communication and lack of understanding? Was it the Africans, who were trying to assert their concept of self, or was it the colonial government, which was trying to enforce its own definition of paternalism? Although

Section 6 of the Native Councils Act of 1943 states, "A council may make provision of facilities for education,"[11] the Africans believed this law embodied an essential element of colonial paternalism and oppression because the schools that emerged operated under strict control of the government in order to fulfill its own political objectives.

This line of thinking was the colonial tradition that the Africans rejected without reservation when, in January 1950, after more than three years of deliberations, the Mangwende Council unanimously passed a resolution to withdraw its application of June 19, 1946, for a government school. Instead, it submitted an application for permission to build its own school without any financial assistance from the government. The council's withdrawal of the application for a government school suggests that it did not accept the reply from Ling as an official government decision. Consequently it did nothing until January 1950, when it withdrew the application. The logic of this technicality angered Huggins and Stark so much that they threatened not to try to solve the problem. However, the threat was a technicality that did not work because the Africans refused to be intimidated.

It is important to note that by January 1950, the Mangwende Council was playing the game according to the rules Huggins and Stark had laid down. Its decision not to accept Ling's reply as a final government decision meant, in effect, that Huggins and Stark would be expected to respond and, thus, forced them to recognize the council as capable of articulating the needs of the people it represented. For quite some time Huggins and Stark appear to have been confused by how well the members of the council understood an issue they presumed they only understood. This was the first time that Huggins and Stark had had to recognize and deal with the thought processes of Africans.

Another aspect of this crisis seems to have caught Huggins and Stark off guard. From the time Ling relayed the denial of the application for a government school to the time that the council submitted an application to build its own school, the Mangwende Council did its homework well to make sure that it understood the issues in dispute. Unaware of the implications of what was happening, Huggins and Stark formed the erroneous impression that the issue was dead. From the legal advice it had received, the council knew there was no basis, except political considerations, for Huggins and Stark to deny the application for a non government school.

With this knowledge, the Mangwende Council began to raise $22,000, the amount it had been advised it would need to begin building the school. It was negotiating with building contractors and consultants on ways of minimizing expenses. The Africans found the idea of a council school so exciting and appealing that Ling began to have some doubts about the wisdom of denying the application for a government school. The enthusiasm and the intense interest with which the Africans pursued this objective and its impact on the conflict between the two sides forced Ling to admit, "So great is the Council's preoccupation with the idea of the council school that all its members think of at present is hoard its funds and aim at building a council school in spite of the large number of mission schools in the Reserve."[12]

Ling knew he had lost any influence he might have had. The Mangwende Council had decided what it and the Africans wanted, thus making him and his role irrelevant. He admitted that he found it "very difficult to lead and advise, the council members think that I am trying to force my ideas on them."[13] For the first time in the history of the colonial government, Ling, Huggins, and Stark recognized the ability of Africans to think critically. They also realized that the Africans wanted to do things according to what they felt was their best interests, not according to the political interests of the colonial bureaucrats. This was a very difficult situation for them to confront.

Therefore, in November 1950, Huggins and Stark instructed Ling to rule that the application for a council-built school was improperly submitted and that it be tabled for six months. The colonial strategy of delaying tactics had come into play. Indeed, there was nothing improper about the manner in which the application was submitted. When the council members tried to argue that the application was properly submitted, Ling overruled them. In May 1951, the six months having barely elapsed, the Mangwende Council voted unanimously to renew its application. The colonial alliance could never admit that its members were frightened by the reality that the application for a council school showed an African understanding of a collective purpose, and that allowing the building of this school would confer on the Africans the kind of power which neither Huggins nor any other colonial official would be able to take away. From the Africans' perspective, accepting the denial of the application for the school would constitute a surrender to political blackmail by the colonial establishment.

Wishing to show that they were in control of the situation, Huggins and Stark put the application for a council school on the shelf for several months. While this indecision dominated their minds, relationships between the two sides continued to deteriorate. The council's refusal to attend to other business until this important issue had been resolved compounded an already bad situation. Fearing that further delay might hurt them in public opinion, Huggins and Stark instructed Ling to advise the council members that a commission of inquiry[14] had been appointed to investigate the character of African education, and that all parties should wait for its report before a decision was made on the application. The council's lack of objection shows its willingness to follow procedures, but the fact that the church organizations were allowed to open new schools during that time caused it to question the government's sincerity.

By giving excuses for delaying and denying approval of the application, Huggins and Stark were playing into the hands of the Africans, because sooner or later they would run out of excuses. All their tactics were designed to condition the Africans to the fact that, in the final analysis, it was the colonial government which must exercise power in all areas of national life. The concept of individual ambition and collective purpose was a dangerous principle to try to apply to colonial settings. That was a type of psychological warfare the Africans knew how to fight. The two sides were poised for a final showdown when in March 1952 the Mangwende Council reactivated its application. But this time Huggins and Stark had an answer, which the members of the Kerr Commission must have had in mind when they recommended that "The extension of council schools must not be artificially hastened, but be sanctioned only in districts where a council is well established."[15] Both sides were pleased, the Mangwende Council members because they had no difficulty meeting the criterion that Kerr thought was important, Huggins and Stark because they thought that it did not, and so once again denied the application.

The Mangwende Council considered this latest response so absurd that its members voted to refuse to accept it. It knew that it had exceeded the minimum requirements by a wide margin. The council challenged Huggins and Stark to offer a more reasonable response or approve the application without further delay. Therefore, in December 1952, the council simply reactivated its application instead of submitting a new one. The application for a council school had gone far beyond the question of education. It had become a struggle between the powerful and the powerless, a fight between the colonizer and the colonized; a confrontation between the forces of colonial oppression and the resources of the oppressed; a test of strength between the desire to perpetuate the colonial condition and the determination to end it. It was, indeed, a battle of wills, a struggle between the strategies of colonial survival and of patience and determination of the Africans.

Huggins and Stark knew that giving in to the African demands would shatter their image as two tough colonial bureaucrats who were determined to remind the Africans of their real place in colonial society. The Africans knew that giving in to this colonial blackmail would destroy the basis of their search for their collective identity. Therefore, they concluded that the longer the impasse continued, the heavier its toll on human relationships and the ability to be rational.

Suddenly, early in 1953, there was an apparent breakthrough. Ling, fearing that he was rapidly losing control of the situation and that the Africans had reduced him to a position of hopelessness and helplessness, took it upon himself to salvage his reputation and restore his relationship with them.

Facing a dilemma he could not easily resolve, he approved the application and recommended it to Huggins and Stark with the comment, "The Council will never be happy until it has its own school."[16] He was obviously caught in the middle of a delicate situation from which there was no escape except to act as he did. In a letter dated May 2, 1953, Stark confirmed that in principle there was no opposition to the council school. When S.E. Morris, the ultra conservative chief native commissioner, realized that he, along with Huggins and Stark, was in a no-win situation, he reluctantly approved the application.

In this set of circumstances the agreement appeared to be sealed. The euphoria with which the Africans celebrated their short-lived victory can be understood in the context of the importance of the council-controlled school, as well as of the impact of the pressure they had applied. At this time, Huggins, facing a declining popularity and confronted by the controversy surrounding his refusal to implement the recommendations of the Kerr Commission, was very much an outsider. All his attention was directed to a campaign for the Federation of Rhodesia and Nyasaland (1953-1963). The head office therefore authorized Morris and Stark to handle the crisis.

To say that there was great excitement in Mangwende Reserve, and all over the country, would be an understatement. The Africans had scored a resounding victory over their colonial master — so they thought — and began to prepare for the beginning of a historic event, unaware that the dream for which they had worked so long and so hard was not to be realized. Meanwhile, throughout the country the Mangwende Rural Council become a shining example of a progressive organization. Africans from all walks of life, old and young, educated and illiterate, rich and poor, professional and ordinary laborers, men and women, rallied around the project with a single mindedness rarely known in the struggle for development in Africa. All other activities were incidental to the building of the council school.

The people in Mangwende had saved money, far more than they needed to build the school. They began to celebrate what they thought would be a great accomplishment, their persistence and determination having paid off. They looked forward to strengthening their council in order to confront the might of the colonial government in the coming struggle. But suddenly there was an unexpected complication. Morris was having second thoughts about approving the building of independent council schools. He now seemed to believe that they would become breeding grounds for subversive activity and anticolonial propaganda along the lines the Mau Mau movement had adopted in Kenya in 1949.[17] But he neglected to consider the real possibility that denial of the application would increase the chances of that happening more than the approval would. After conferring, Morris and Stark decided to demand full particulars about the proposed school.

The Crisis Moves to a Head: Stark and Ling Take Permanent Leave

The Mangwende Council saw this demand as a colonial strategy to find an excuse to rescind the approval of its application. It remains a matter of speculation as to what would have happened if the council had furnished the details that Morris and Stark had requested. The council, fearing that doing so would give the colonial government more power than it needed, declined to do so. Instead, it voted unanimously, after a debate, to ask Chief Mangwende to lead a delegation to Harare for a meeting with Stark and Morris. Huggins's successor, Garfield Todd, felt that he was not familiar enough with the details of this complex issue, and asked Stark and Morris to handle it. This decision proved to be a major error. Nothing came of this meeting with the Mangwende delegation except charges and counter charges. Mistrust and bitterness dominated the meeting, with each side accusing the other of behaving in a manner unbecoming the position of responsible officials.

When Todd expressed some sympathy for the African position, Stark felt that he had lost the support he had enjoyed under Huggins, and therefore took permanent leave, distraught, frustrated, and embittered. The 20 years for which he had faithfully served his government appeared to have accomplished little. When H.C. Finkle succeeded Stark in 1954, the Africans thought that there was a new atmosphere of racial understanding might offer both sides an opportunity to resolve the issue satisfactorily, and allow the council to build its own school. Huggins and Stark, who represented the old colonial attitude and behavior toward Africans, were out of the scene. Todd and Finkle were both men of considerable understanding and moderate views. They therefore felt that since their application had already been approved, it was simply a matter of making it official.

But Morris, an old ally of both Huggins and Stark, soon emerged to exert more influence than Todd and Finkle because he and Ling were more familiar with the crisis. Because he thought Ling's continued presence on the scene would make it difficult to resolve this crisis, Morris recommended replacing him with C.C. Meredith, a man of extreme racial views. Morris and Meredith began to revive the old rules of playing the colonial game. In early 1955, Meredith informed the Mangwende Council that a new educational plan for Africans[18] was being developed and that it would not permit the building of council schools. This was a devastating blow.

There is no doubt that Meredith was appointed because he had the reputation of a colonial hard-liner. But in holding the views that he did, he became a victim of the colonial psychology which was the hallmark of Huggins and Stark. A tough colonialist who believed that Africans must be reminded of their proper place in colonial society, Meredith had neither the understanding of Ling nor the patience of Finkle. He was an official who accomplished his tasks by threatening to use force. Because the Africans held Meredith personally responsible for this latest colonial charade, they went out of their way to discredit him and label any projects he tried to fulfill as deliberately calculated to inflict the severest damage possible to their cause. They launched a campaign to make his work impossible, to sabotage it wherever possible. Soon rhetoric turned into physical violence, and a general breakdown of law and order became so pervasive that all government operations came to a halt, not only in Mangwende Reserve but throughout the country.

This was the environment in which Chief Mangwende's submerged resistance gave way to open defiance, in the belief that the council's application for its own school could not be withdrawn without inflicting severe damage on the African struggle for self. Meredith could not ignore what he regarded as a challenge to his authority. In the context of the political activity during that time, Chief Mangwende found an appropriate forum in which to challenge not only Meredith as native commissioner for the reserve but also the colonial government itself. The issue of the council application for a school was set aside as the strategy for political struggle took center stage. Huggins's and Stark's legacy was now having its ultimate effect as Africans throughout the country and the colonial government engaged in a bitter and brutal struggle for survival.

Utilizing the the declaration of a state of emergency that Edgar Whitehead[19] made on February 28, 1959, Morris and Meredith recommended mass arrests of African political activists and their leaders, and that Chief Mangwende be banned from his area for life. On January 14, 1960, Morris, with Whitehead's approval,[20] issued a statement explaining why the chief was removed from office and banned:

> Over the past five years this Chief's behavior has been increasingly obstructive and detrimental to good order. His behavior has paralyzed the operation of the Mangwende Reserve Native Council and recently led a delegation to Salisbury to demand that the Council be abolished. The government would no longer tolerate his behavior and has removed him from office.[21]

If Morris's statement was a correct example of how the colonial government did things, and one is persuaded to believe that it was, then there is little surprise that the Africans felt a sense of urgency to end the colonial condition. Morris knew that at no time had the chief tried to abolish the council.

All he had done was to respond to the request of council members, by discussion and vote, to lead a delegation to a meeting with government officials to resolve the issues that had been neglected for many years. The real usurpers of power were Morris, Meredith, and the system they represented.

The Brown Commission in Perspective: Schemes of Misunderstanding

The reality of this tragic situation compelled Whitehead, as required by the British government, to appoint James Brown chairman of a five-member commission on October 28, 1960, to investigate the issue of why "there is discontent prevailing in the Mangwende Reserve and why there is deterioration in the cooperation of the inhabitants of the Reserve with the authority."[22] Like the Kerr Commission of 1951, the Brown Commission revealed some disturbing things about the character of the colonial government. Among the issues it discussed were three that were the major cause of this conflict: the Native Councils Act, the behavior of colonial officials, and the application for a council school. In concluding that, by assuming the chairmanship of Mangwende Council, Meredith had gone far beyond the provision of the Native Councils Act, the Brown Commission suggested that the arrogance which influenced his official conduct "lay at the root of the unhappy conflict between the people of Mangwende and their white superiors."[23] The Brown Commission further concluded that because of the provisions of this law, Meredith placed himself in a situation of conflict of interest: serving the interests of the government he represented and serving the interests of the people he was appointed to serve.

Addressing the question of the school controversy, the Brown Commission concluded, "If there was a need for the Department of Native Education to give what the African people need in this most important area of their life, it is now,"[24] and went on to add that the school would have given the Africans a fulfillment of their aspirations, a feeling of belonging, and a sense of accomplishment. For the government to deny the application was to play a political power game that only benefited the Africans in the long run. The Brown Commission sounded like the Kerr Commission when it unhesitatingly castigated Meredith for showing "a grave underestimation of the imperative nature of change and the ability of the Africans to understand it. Even well-prepared schemes may lead to misunderstanding, resentment and disruption of life when too little attention is paid to the human factor."[25]

The Brown Commission seemed to understand how the nature and the extent of the concept of change affected the Africans in a way similar to that of Harold Macmillan, the British prime minister from 1957 to 1963. When he delivered a speech to the joint session of the South African Parliament during a grand tour of Africa a few months before the Brown Commission submitted its report, he said: "The wind of change is blowing through the continent [of Africa]. Whether we like it or not the growth of national consciousness is a political fact. We must all accept it as a fact, and our national policies must take account of it.''[26]

Finally, arguing that the government must not seek to exploit Chief Mangwende because his influence was likely to increase as a result, the Brown Commission recommended that it was in the interest of the government itself to restore him to his position of chief: He still commands the loyalty of many if not most of the people in Mangwende Reserve among whom there is a widespread belief that he was deposed for reasons other than for his role in the school controversy.''[27] Whitehead's refusal to accept this recommendation shows how accurate the Brown Commission's conclusion was.

Summary and Conclusion

To conclude that the report of the Brown Commission was shattering for Whitehead, Morris, and Meredith is to suggest that the colonial government had learned little from the report of the Kerr Commission. There is no doubt that the Brown Commission pinpointed the objective of the colonial government as controlling the educational development of Africans as the major cause of the conflict between itself and the Africans when it concluded that the school controversy was only a symptom of a deeper conflict caused by the colonial condition. But, like the Kerr Commission, in all that it said against the continuation of this colonial condition, the Brown Commission did not have the courage to address the hard reality that the Africans saw their struggle for educational advancement as synonymous with their struggle for political independence. The school controversy became a visible symbol of that struggle. Huggins, Stark, Morris, and Meredith knew that this was the essence of the conflict.

The surprising thing in all this is that Huggins refused to acknowledge that the law his administration enacted in 1937, and amended in 1943, had by 1952 become the main instrument with which both sides launched their campaign, Huggins to prove that the Africans were unable to understand the nature of their advancement and the Africans to prove that they could articulate their needs in a broader social order than the limitations imposed by the colonial condition. Clearly, this conflict was a struggle between an effort to perpetuate the colonial condition and an effort to end it.

True, the Africans lost an opportunity to build and operate their own school. But what they gained from this loss was a realization that as long as the colonial condition remained, they would be denied a real opportunity for advancement. That was an education far more important than the one the colonial government could give them. What the colonial government lost was the opportunity to take the Africans into its confidence and to create a new environment of mutual racial understanding. This was what made the war of independence beginning, in 1966, a particularly brutal one. This was why many whites decided to leave the country when a black government was formed on April 18, 1980.

There is no question that this crisis had its origin in the policies Huggins and Stark had pursued over two decades. What colonial official wanted to be the first to accommodate the demands of the colonized in a way that suggested a loss of his power? Because Huggins and Stark resigned when they could not face the seriousness of the problems they had created, Whitehead, Morris, and Meredith found themselves in a situation far more serious than that of Huggins and Stark. When the Rhodesia Front assumed office in December 1962, the relationships between Africans and the government had been so badly damaged that they could not be repaired. The only way to resolve the problem was a military struggle.

The crisis arising from the legacy that Huggins and Stark had left in their educational policies was now at its peak, and the last of the colonial government officials were reaping what their predecessors had sown many years before. Chapter 8 will attempt to summarize Stark's work in the context of three essential elements that heavily influenced his philosophy of education for Africans and the policies he pursued. The work of the Western missionaries, the psychology of the colonial officials, and the rise of African consciousness.

Notes

1. The Report of the Commission of Inquiry into Discontent in the Mangwende Reserve, James Brown, Chairman, 1961, p. 5.
2. Godfrey Huggins, during a debate on a bill to amend the Native Councils Act of 1937., in Southern Rhodesia, Legislative Debates, June 26, 1941., p. 221
3. Ibid., p. 225.
4. The Report of the Brown Commission, p. 41.
5. Each church-related school first admitted students of its own denomination. This means that students whose parents were not members of any denomination would find it hard to be admitted into any of the schools. Mangwende Rural Council thought that this was discrimination based on religion.
6. The Report of the Brown Commission, para. 91, p. 40
7. Southern Rhodesia, Ordinance Number 7: Ordinance to Provide for the Control of Native Schools, July 19, 1912. The effect of this legislation on African educational development was discussed in Chapter 1 of this volume.
8. Ian Smith, the last colonial prime minister, who served from April 13, 1964, to March 3, 1979, told the author during an interview on July 20, 1983, that the civil war actually started in 1962, as soon as his Rhodesia Front Party won the elections held in December of that year. Dispute of historical facts aside, Smith blamed Huggins for his own problems.
9. The Report of the Brown Commission, para. 185, p. 77.
10. Ibid., para. 119, p. 48.
11. Southern Rhodesia, Native Council Act, Section 6, 1943.
12. Ibid., para. 191, p. 79.
13. Ibid., para. 191, p. 80.
14. The Kerr Commission, discussed in Chapter 6 of this volume.
15. The The Report of the Kerr Commission, para. 282, p. 45.
16. Ibid., para. 194, p. 81.
17. Ibid., para. 197, p. 81.
18. The Five-Year Education Plan, which Todd announced in 1956 in an effort to initiate a crash program to undo the damage he believed Huggins and Stark had inflicted on African education during the 20 years which they were in power.
19. Prime minister of Colonial Zimbabwe from February 17, 1958, to December 16, 1962.
20. Todd had suffered a humiliating defeat in the elections held on February 16, 1958, due to his apparent lack of decisiveness on issues of national importance.
21. S.E. Morris, chief native commissioner, in a statement issued to explain the reasons for the deposition and deportation of Chief Mangwende, January 14, 1960. In the Zimbabwe National Archives.
22. The Report of the Brown Commission, p. iii.
23. Ibid., para 380, p. 160.
24. Ibid., para. 449, p. 186.
25. Ibid., p. 450, p. 187.
26. Harold Macmillan, "Commonwealth Independence and Interdependence," an address to the Joint Session of the South African Parliament, February 3, 1960.
27. The Report of the Brown Commission, para. 321, p. 135.

8
Educational Policy for Africans under Stark: Summary, Conclusion, and Implications

The doctrine of racial discrimination is based upon our belief that there are unchangeable differences between the races which cannot be reconciled.
— Godfrey Huggins, 1954

The Africans needed to understand that academic education is not for everyone.
— Ian Smith, 1983

Stark's Work in Perspective

The purpose of this study is to examine the effect of the philosophy George Stark formulated as director of native education from 1934 to 1954, and the policy he designed relative to the education of Africans. The conclusion reached from the evidence presented is that in those two decades the implementation of his policy did more harm than good to the educational development of Africans. With his uncompromising belief in practical training, and his commitment to meet the labor requirements of the colonial industries, Stark sacrificed a good academic education for the Africans, and thus handicapped their development.

It has also been concluded that Stark was a product of the conditions of the times, his values influencing his ideas. The fact that at first he took orders from his superiors suggests the structured hierarchical order under which he functioned. By 1936, however, only a year after he was confirmed as permanent director of native education, he and Godfrey Huggins had entered into an alliance that compelled them to depend on each other for political survival. The destiny of one became inseparable from that of the other. The fate of the one sealed that of the other.

The question which one must ask is: How did it happen that two men were brought together to develop identical policy from identical philosophies? The answer lies in the times from which they came. Huggins, a medical doctor by training, came to Zimbabwe in 1911 from Britain and abandoned his profession in order to devote his life to ensuring that whites continued to exercise total control over Africans. Stark, a teacher, came to Zimbabwe in 1929 from Lovedale, a Church of Scotland school for Africans in South Africa.

One would have thought that Stark's experience at Lovedale would have prepared him to appreciate the problems that Africans in colonial Zimbabwe were experiencing better than Huggins, who never had an opportunity to interact with them, and so never came to understand and appreciate their needs. We have concluded that Huggins and Stark failed to see these problems from their proper perspective because they based their policies on their philosophy. That philosophy was based on Victorian principles which stated that the only form of education from which Africans could benefit was manual labor and practical training.

The underlying principle of this belief was that Africans could more readily acquire basic elements of Western civilization by imitating whites things that were practical than by any other means. Throughout their careers, both men operated under this belief, and there was nothing that anyone could have done to help them understand the broader aspect of African education.

In order to understand why Huggins and Stark pursued the policies they did, one needs to understand the context in which they formulated them. They did not believe Africans were less than human, but that they possessed an intellect decidedly less than that of whites. This was one of the major components of the Victorian view of Africans, and Huggins and Stark operated by it. There were three environmental factors in Stark's formulation of his policies: the character of the Western missionary, the psychology of the colonial government officials, and the rise of African consciousness. Let us discuss each, to show how it influenced Stark's philosophy and policies.

The Character of the Missionary: Preaching Biblical Christianity or Western Culture?

From the time Robert Moffat founded the first formal school for Africans at Inyati in 1859, the major objective of Western missionaries was to convert Africans to Christianity. There was nothing wrong with this objective in itself. That was how the Romans had promoted their culture. But what was questionable about the work of Western missionaries in nineteenth century Africa was that they equated Christianity with Western culture — they seemed to confuse the teaching of biblical Christianity with the practices of Western culture.

For Western missionaries to persuade Africans to embrace the ideals of Christianity was, in essence, to ask them to discard their own culture as a condition of acceptance into the Christian community. In failing to appreciate the positive attributes of African culture, the missionaries made it hard for the two cultural groups to create the environment of understanding that biblical Christianity promoted. This is why Africans largely rejected missionary education, an action that Moffat, Livingstone, and their colleagues deeply regretted but did not fully understand. If they had understood why Africans were rejecting their form of teaching, they would have designed a strategy different from the one they were using.

Methodist Bishop Ralph Dodge, who served as a missionary to Africa from 1936 to 1972, discussed the negative impact of Victorian missionaries on the colonization of Africa when he wrote:

> The participation of the Church in the slave trade and its unwillingness at critical times to identify itself with the indigenous people, made it often considered a European colonial institution. This situation was accentuated by close identification of the Church with European colonial governments.[1]

What Dodge says can be supported by specific examples. In 1888, when King Lobengula was under pressure from Rhodes to grant him exclusive mining rights, he enlisted Rev. Charles Helm, who, like Moffat and Livingstone, was a member of the London Missionary Society, to act as both his adviser and his interpreter, totally unaware that Helm was in the service of Rhodes to spy on the king so that more effective plans could be made to colonize his land.[2] As late as 1965, when Africans were designing a strategy to fight against colonialism, it was widely reported that some missionaries were spying on them and joining the colonial army against the people they claimed they were in Zimbabwe to serve.

This kind of behavior made the Africans believe that Western missionaries were preaching the gospel of Western cultural superiority, not biblical Christianity. By the time the colonial government was officially established in 1890, the partnership between the colonialists and the missionaries had been so strengthened that the Africans saw little difference between them. The missionaries' failure to protest or to oppose Earl Grey's characterization (1896) of Africans as needing nothing more than manual labor as a viable form of education shows the extent to which they supported the colonial establishment.

Difficult as it was to do, the Victorian missionaries eventually recognized that their acquiescence to the colonial policy had cost them dearly. The racially discriminatory character of the Education Ordinance of 1899 and its subsequent amendments, especially Ordinance Number 7 of 1912, alerted them to the danger to come. This awareness made it possible for them to change their strategy from supporting the colonial government to advocating a genuine improvement of Africans through adequate education.

For example, from 1912 until 1921, Reverend John Harris of the London Aborigines Protection Society immersed himself in the activities of the colonial government, especially in its policy towards the Africans, unwilling to accept any decision or the implementation of any policy in which he or his representative had not been involved. On October 27, 1921, Premier Charles Coghlan wrote a letter to his successor, Howard Moffat, to say that Reverend Harris was to be present at all meetings where issues affecting Africans were being discussed.[3] One can argue that the missionaries were doing this not so much because they thought the government was pursuing a wrong policy as because they wanted the Africans to believe they were their true allies in their struggle for development.

Another question must be asked: At what point did the missionaries realize that their support of the colonial government's educational policy was pursuing was not the right thing to do? Although it is hard to fix a specific date, 1899 seemed to signal a change of position by the missionaries. The formation of the Southern Rhodesia Christian Conference in 1906 demonstrates that the missionaries and the colonial establishment no longer espoused the same view regarding the education of the Africans. The colonial government wanted them to train as cheap laborers, but the missionaries wanted something better. In 1928, for example, Rev. T.A. O'Farrell of the Methodist Church explained the importance of educating Africans beyond practical training: "The leaders whom we are developing today may become the pilots of their race in far larger areas than Rhodesia."[4]

The missionaries' wanting an education for Africans better than practical training explains two things. The first is that until 1946, African education was their exclusive domain. The second is that the missionaries were the first to raise the importance of post primary education for Africans. The opening of St. Augustine's Secondary School in 1939 demonstrates their desire for the Africans to be educated beyond the rudiments of elementary education and practical training. All these developments had the cumulative effect of influencing the missionaries over an extended period of time to conclude that Africans needed a better education than the colonial government was prepared to offer them.

We must now ask another question about the character of the missionaries relative to their role in the Africans' educational development. Why did they want Africans to have a better education than practical training? The answer lies in their desire that the Africans be able to read and to write so that they could understand religious literature and interpret its meaning according to Christian precepts. They considered basic literacy insufficient to accomplish this task. The process of acquiring this kind of education required an environment different from what the colonial government wanted. Earl Grey recognized this in 1896 when he opposed a rigorous religious education because he argued that its ultimate effect was to broaden the Africans' minds in such a way that they would begin to understand their condition of life in a much broader context. Reverend O'Farrell's comments in 1928 on the importance of training Africans for broader leadership role in their country did not represent a view that the colonial government shared at any time. In fact, the colonial government would never change its policy of practical training until its end in 1979. It is therefore not surprising that as soon as Stark was appointed acting director of Native Education 1934, there was immediately an environment of institutional conflict that reached an unprecedented crisis in 1970.

But along with the positive side of the missionary role in African education came a negative side. In pursuing an educational policy that did not emanate from a collective definition of objectives, from a partnership with the Africans themselves, the educational process had serious limitations. The missionaries did not realize that only an education designed to fulfill the needs of the individual students fulfilled those of society. Missionary education failed to accommodate this fundamental principle, and thus Africans were reluctant to accept it for many years following the opening of Inyati in 1859. They thought it was being used to persuade them to discard their cultural traditions. For this reason Africans' negative response to missionary education remained a problem until 1920.

The error committed by Reverend Harris and Reverend O'Farrell, as well as other missionaries of the twentieth century, was their conclusion that because the Africans reacted negatively to their religious educational policy, they were unable to understand the basic elements of Western education, which they equated with Christianity. This erroneous conception was adopted by the colonial government as an important feature of its standardized policy. Clearly, then, the missionary desire to convert the Africans to Christianity was a cultural objective that could not be altered, and missionary teaching and African learning were intended to fulfill this objective. In the nineteenth century those Africans who refused to accept Christianity were considered to have refused a generous offer of education. The reverse was also true:

Those Africans who accepted Western education were considered to have accepted Christianity.

This is why the more the missionaries pursued their educational policy of persuading the Africans to accept Christianity, the more the Africans resisted. Because the Africans were afraid that accepting Christianity would threaten the essential features of their own culture, they did not think the education the missionaries were trying to persuade them to accept had any practical value for their lives.[5] But all this would change in the twentieth century, and while the missionaries were able to adjust to new conditions, the colonial government was not. If any aspect of missionary educational programs had a profound influence on George Stark's philosophy, it was the thinking that was gaining ground by the time he was appointed in 1934: that the Africans must receive an education better than industrial training. A fervent colonialist, Stark saw this thinking as the ultimate threat to the whites' position of power.

Stark was so rigid because he did not want to be the first colonial official to preside over the transformation of a system that he believed had worked well since the enactment of the Education Ordinance of 1899. This explains his determination to win the confidence of the missionaries after Jowitt's resignation, but they did not have confidence in him. This study has furnished evidence to show that the level of mistrust between Stark and the missionaries steadily intensified over the years as the position of the missionaries changed. Therefore, Stark designed his policy as he did partly to assert his authority over the missionaries and partly to remind the Africans of their proper place in colonial society.

The Psychology of the Colonial Officials

A phenomenon that has been an intriguing aspect of the colonial government's educational policy for Africans is the manner in which it assumed the responsibility for designing it. Its entering the educational arena in 1899 was the sequel to major events that began with the so-called Rudd Concession of October, 1888. The colonization of Zimbabwe in September 1890, the overthrow and assassination of King Lobengula in 1893, the promulgation of the Orders in Council of 1894, and the bitter war of 1896-1897, all combined to produce a set of circumstances that played into the hands of the colonial zealots.

In entering the arena of educational policy for Africans, the colonial government thought that it would succeed where the missionaries had failed. It saw its triumph over the Africans in these events as a triumph over adversity and as a demonstration of superiority. It was unaware that it would face problems far more serious than the ones the missionaries faced. The psychology of the colonial officials did not prepare them for what was to come. The primary purpose of the colonization of Zimbabwe, as was that of other territories in Africa by European nations, was to secure the raw materials that could improve the standard of living the Industrial Revolution made possible. The utilization of Africans as cheap laborers would make it possible for the colonial entrepreneurs to make huge profits from their business ventures.

But the colonial establishment quickly learned that for the Africans to function effectively as cheap laborers, they needed some form of training. Training entailed an educational process. It concluded that the Africans must receive an education quite different from the kind that the missionaries were persuading them to accept.[6] This strategy created a dilemma for the colonial government: to develop a viable educational policy for the Africans and face the real danger of awakening their self-consciousness, or to deny them that kind of education and limit their ability to function effectively as laborers. The colonial government pondered this dilemma for three years beginning with the end of the war in 1897, totally unable to decide, clear only in its desire to design a policy different from that of the missionaries. The damage the war had done to race, relations which proved not to be undone for the remainder of the colonial rule, complicated the colonial process of formulating educational policy.

However, the need for cheap labor outweighed all other considerations. In its initial stage, the colonial government counted on support from the missionaries by making aid grants available to schools they operated, provided the education they offered was simple practical training and manual labor only. This is the kind of cooperation the Graham Commission of 1911, the Hadfield Commission of 1927, the Barnes Commission of 1929, and the Kerr Commission of 1951 all recommended, not only in order to improve the education of Africans along the lines of practical training but also to give credibility to the colonial government itself at a time when doubts were being expressed about its motives.

It is also important to remember that in considering its move, the colonial government believed that while the educational policy of the missionaries was intended to "stabilize the faith of converts and assist in Christian character development,"[7] it was not designed to train them as laborers. The colonial government needed cheap labor more than it needed anything else from the Africans.[8] Slowly the difference in the educational policy pursued by the missionaries and that pursued by the colonial government placed the two white institutions at a crossroads. Conflict steadily increased and hindered their ability to see the importance of developing African education from the perspective of its value to their own advancement as the best means of ensuring the future of the whites.

Grey seemed unaware of this ultimate consequence of colonial educational policy because he and other colonial officials were preoccupied with producing cheap labor and tried to do every thing possible to ensure a steady supply. But no matter how much the government tried, it did not always succeed. In his report for 1898-1900 Grey recognized the lack of interest among Africans in working for whites as a major problem of the labor supply:

> The dearth may be ascribed to two causes. The well-being of the Natives due to the abundance of crops and the low rate of the hut tax which they are asked to pay. Self — discipline and self-control are unknown among the Natives. Through forced labor it is possible to inculcate work habits and make them useful members of society.[9]

Indeed, forced labor remained an essential component of colonial policy toward the Africans until 1943, the year Huggins amended the Native Councils Act of 1937.

The views Grey and his associates in the colonial government expressed, and the educational policy they formulated, were part of popular Victorian thinking among the whites, which regarded Africans as inferior. As the myth went, they were destined to carry out the orders of their white superiors. Grey himself fully endorsed this kind of thinking.[10] In this attitude lay the tragedy of the colonial educational policy in Zimbabwe. Having recognized that the hut tax of 1894 had failed to induce the Africans to work for the whites, Grey laid the foundation of the Education Ordinance that his successor, William Milton,[11] pushed through the legislature in 1899.

The major provision of the Education Ordinance of 1899 was an aid grant of $4.00 per school per white student who had met an academic standard and $1.00 per school per African student who had met industrial training criteria. However, the missionaries were reluctant to apply for aid grants because of their belief that the new ordinance was discriminatory against African students. They were also uncomfortable with the educational process itself, not because they believed the Africans were entitled to equal educational opportunity but because they feared they would lose the freedom they had enjoyed prior to the implementation of the aid grants with their restrictive strings.[12]

When, in 1901, three African schools with a total enrollment of 265 students received a total of $638.40, the colonial government believed it had succeeded where the missionaries had failed: implementing a policy consistent with its objective of producing cheap laborers. But it had created a set of new problems would lead to serious institutional conflict. Not only did the government demand that manual labor form the major thrust of African education as a condition of receiving the grants, but it also demanded to inspect the schools, to ensure that its policy was being implemented in the way it was intended. The inspection report that George Duthie submitted following his visit to St. Augustine's School on November 26, 1901, is a testimony to the successful implementation of that policy. Practical training and manual labor, considered a viable education for Africans, had become a religion, fervently practiced by the colonial establishment by the time that Stark assumed office in 1934.

Encouraged by the results of the exercise of power the aid grants had suddenly given it in formulating its educational policy for Africans, the colonial government enacted a series of amendments between 1902 and 1912 further to strengthen its hand in forcing the policy of industrial training and manual labor. For instance, the Education Ordinance of 1907 divided all African schools into divisions called classes. The colonial educational policy from 1907 to 1927 coincided with many political and socioeconomic developments. The Rolin Report of 1913, the outbreak of war in 1914, the outbreak of influenza in 1918, and the national referendum in 1923 all came to mean one important thing in African education: emphasis on training Africans as cheap laborers. The opening of Domboshawa in 1920 and Tjolotjo in 1921 gave impetus to a momentum that was already gathering speed.

All these events were leading to a climax in 1927: the establishment of the Department of Native Education under Harold Jowitt, an intellectual who was a misfit within the hierarchy of the colonial structure. Worse still, Jowitt was a liberal in the mold of Ray Stockil, a life-long political opponent of Godfrey Huggins. That Stockil's views were similar to those of J. C. Smuts, the South African military and political leader, and those of Robert Tredgold, chief justice of the High Court whose decisions often contradicted Huggins's laws, especially in cases involving Africans, suggests that Jowitt had supporters in high places. This was a strategy that Stark would later use effectively.

One must therefore see Jowitt's work in light of the political views of the leaders at the time. Charles Coghlan, Howard Moffat, Ray Stockil, and George Mitchell were thinkers representing a small segment of a white population who felt that for the whites to have a future in Zimbabwe, they had an obligation to promote the advancement of the Africans. Jowitt's membership in this group was no accident, and in seven years he vigorously pursued a policy that meant the introduction of practical training must steadily give way to the introduction of a good academic education. But the circumstances that brought the political career of Howard Moffat and George Mitchell to a sudden end in 1933 also brought to a sudden end the promising policies of Harold Jowitt in 1934. Godfrey Huggins's vigorous campaign vigorously on an anti-African platform led him to regard his victory in the elections of 1933 as a clear mandate to reverse the policies that Mitchell and Jowitt were pursuing. George Stark, who joined the Department of Native Education in 1929 at the invitation of Jowitt, assumed the directorship of African education at a very critical stage in the development of the Africans of Zimbabwe. For two decades, Huggins and Stark operated under the Victorian belief that Africans must be trained to function only as laborers.

One must be careful to portray Stark not as a callous colonial bureaucrat who assigned himself the role of a fall guy or a lone ranger, but as an agent through whom Huggins lived out his philosophy of the place of Africans in colonial society. Unfortunately, he was no less visible than Huggins. Huggins and Stark had a symbiotic relationships. Each needed the other to survive in an increasingly hostile environment. Thus, Huggins, late in his political career, had the confidence to define the relationship between Africans and whites as synonymous with the relationship between horse and rider. But in this symbiotic relationship, Huggins and Stark sealed their own fate.

Once Huggins and Stark decided they wanted to pursue a policy of practical training for Africans, they could not reverse or amend it without facing political consequences. But in pursuing that policy, they left themselves open to severe criticism that they were following a back door route to the economic and social enslavement of Africans. Successful as they claimed to be in the pursuit of their policy, Huggins and Stark remained tragic figures in the political arena of colonial Zimbabwe. Their legacy was the bitter fruit their successors harvested.

The Rise of African Consciousness

The formation in 1933, the year Huggins came to power, of the first African National Congress (ANC) under the brilliant leadership of Aaron Jacha was an event destined to alter the course of colonial politics and eventually to set the stage for an independent state under an African government. While how this happened is outside the scope of this study, the evidence discussed shows how the rise of African consciousness forced this to come about. Although this was a hard road that took many years to travel and involved untold hardships, the ANC piloted the rise of consciousness among Africans in a way Huggins and Stark failed to understand. Indeed, they would never fully understand many aspects of African life.

Although the ANC faded away with the beginning of the war in 1939, it had implanted in Africans an awareness that their own destiny, in a world controlled by the whites, was in their own hands. The conference of African leaders held in London at the conclusion of the war in 1945, the year of the Asquith Report, was invigorating and rejuvenated the consciousness that had lived in the hearts of Africans throughout the war years. From 1945, this new consciousness rose so rapidly that it enabled the Africans to recognize the policy pursued by Huggins and Stark for what it was: a prescription that had to be eliminated if the future was to be meaningful.

The year 1945 seems crucial to the rise of African consciousness in many ways. This study has concluded that some leading white liberals felt that conditions had changed and that it was time for the whites to recognize the rights of the Africans as equals. One such person was J. C. Smuts, prime minister of South Africa from 1939 to 1948. Speaking at a banquet held in his honor by the governor-general of Mozambique in April, 1945, Smuts argued and warned:

> There is room for white and black to live side by side. Neither is independent of the other. By their labor the Natives have provided the great progress which, in a space of a generation, has transformed the face of this vast area. The white man's place in Africa depends on a modus vivendi based on justice and granting the Native people opportunities for development.[13]

This liberal view must be seen in the context of other developments at the time. A day earlier, Aldon Mwamuka, president of the African Teachers Association in Zimbabwe, at the annual conference held in Mutare, had addressed the same issue that Smuts discussed: the importance of granting equal educational opportunity to Africans as a means of eliminating possible racial conflict. In his address Mwamuka had two messages, one for the colonial government and one for his fellow Africans.

In a message intended for the ears of the colonial officials Mwamuka observed,

> During the war we have been called upon to assist in every way possible to fight against the forces of darkness, tyranny, and racism. Our men in the Rhodesia African Rifles are shedding blood in order that men everywhere may be free from racial domination. They are dying so that the world may be a place where a man is not denied the full scope of his ability because he is black.[14]

Mwamuka's message to his fellow Africans was as powerful as it was clear:

> Let our behavior and our teaching be such that our pupils may go out of our schools as men and women who are ambassadors of the light and model of good citizenship that members on the other side of the color line may have no cause to deny us those things which, as members of the human family, are ours as well.[15]

In order for this to happen, Mwamuka urged the colonial government to provide the Africans an education different from that which Huggins and Stark had been providing since 1934. This could be done only by a total equality between the students of both races. As Mwamuka saw it, total equality meant one thing: integration of the schools. Huggins and Stark's failure to accept the wisdom of this line of thinking suggests the danger of the course they had charted since 1934.

For the Africans to feel the detrimental effects of colonialism was to recognize its oppressive nature. What Smuts and Mwamuka said constitute graphic examples of the powerful influence of the rise of African consciousness. Thus, by 1950 the Africans were rejecting Huggins's racial philosophy and his definition of partnership as the same thing as the relationship between horse and rider. The Africans' ability to raise questions about the colonial imposition was the first step in recognizing that Huggins and Stark represented an oppressive institution that had to be eliminated if other forms of development were to take place. The Africans also knew that without good academic education, there was no development in any other direction. These were the dimensions of the rise of African consciousness that made it possible for the Africans to see the Huggins-Stark alliance from the perspective of its negative impact on their quest for self and its limiting effect on their struggle for advancement.

If Huggins and Stark's efforts to manipulate the education of Africans proved them to be shrewd colonial politicians, they also showed them to be the high priests of miscalculation of the African resentment of their policies. There is no question that they misjudged the Africans' rising consciousness and incorrectly measured the pulse of public reaction to their objectives. When the Methodist Church issued a statement on February 9, 1946, calling for a change in their educational policy, and when Garfield Todd in 1947 suggested the appointment of a commission of inquiry into African education, Huggins and Stark felt that these suggestions belonged in the wastepaper basket. Thus, the two men began to lay the foundation of their political mausoleum.

Summary and Implications: Stark's Legacy in Perspective

This study has furnished evidence to lead to the conclusion that as director of native education from 1934 to 1954, George Stark operated under a set of principles that the colonial government formulated for the first time in 1899. The demand for cheap labor, combined with the Victorian negative perception of Africans, forced him to conclude that because they were considered inferior, the only form of education for Africans was practical training and manual labor. By the time Stark assumed office, this erroneous perception had become something of an accepted fact. Throughout the 20 years that he was in office, Stark, like Huggins, was unable to adjust his philosophy to suit the conditions of the times.Even after the end of the war, when many influential whites were advocating a change of attitude, Stark remained loyal to an old myth.

When the Kerr Commission identified racial discrimination in the educational process as the major problem in the educational development of Africans,[16] Huggins defended it: "The doctrine of racial discrimination is based upon our belief that there are certain unchangeable differences between the races which cannot be reconciled."[17]

This attitude had serious implications for the educational policies of future colonial governments. Three of Huggins's four successors — Edgar Whitehead, Winstone Field, and Ian Smith — tried to use the racial philosophy and policies that he left behind. The only exception was Garfield Todd, who tried to make a major effort to improve the education of Africans. But he paid a heavy price, a humiliating defeat in the general elections of 1958.

In trying to sustain both the racial philosophy and the policies Huggins had put in place over two decades, Whitehead, Field, and Smith experienced the ire of the African determination and the full weight of the rise of African consciousness. The bitter civil war that lasted from 1966 to 1979 could have been avoided if Smith had chosen to abandon that philosophy and those policies. Unfortunately, he believed that he had inherited it from Huggins as a legacy from Rhodes, whose discipleship he believed he must protect.

This is the context in which Smith made the following statement to this author during an interview in Harare, in 1983:

> We recognized that here was a gap between the education of the white students and the African students. This was part of our history, it was not due to anything that we did. Before the war the Africans did not believe in education because they thought that it was something that belonged to the white man. But after the war there was a sudden surge and the Africans wanted education. Therefore, the government of Sir Godfrey Huggins had a major problem in providing necessary facilities. But the Africans needed to understand that academic education is not for everyone.[18]

Smith's attempt to adhere to the policies Huggins had used shows how strongly he believed in them. It is sad that neither man recognized what President Franklin Roosevelt said in 1938: that no people can be kept eternally ignorant nor eternally enslaved. The lack of knowledge about the harmful effects of the colonial condition was the tragedy of the legacy of the policies that Stark pursued under Huggins. Smith, as a claimed successor to Huggins, paid the ultimate price.

The reality of the legacy of Stark's educational policy is profoundly felt in Zimbabwe in other important respects. For example, a senior teacher at George Stark Secondary School in Harare (opened in 1955 as a primary school for Africans) told the author during a visit to the school in 1989:

> A few years ago, the white headmaster if the school pulled down the framed photograph of George Stark from a prominent position it had been hanging in the school, removed it from its frame, and pinned it on a bulletin board in an obscure room. This pseudo white Zimbabwean nationalist then argued that the educational policy that Stark pursued contributed greatly to the problems that we are now facing in this country.[19]

What can be learned from this tragic situation is that the colonial condition will not last forever. Even the Roman Empire rose and fell. But what may last longer than the physical presence of colonial government is its residual effects. In this regard, African nations have been the victims. The emergence of various forms of government, such as one-party rule or one-man rule, erodes the individual ambition and the collective purpose, both of which are essential ingredients of national development, and replaces them with the government's own definition of what national progress is. This is still hurting many countries in Africa today.

In addition, there is the question of the educational process itself. The officials who succeeded the colonial governments in Africa have, in many respects, adopted their strategies for the sole purpose of keeping themselves in office at the expense of the educational development of their people.The curricular structure and the methods of administration in some countries of Africa have remained the same as they were during the colonial period. This is why illiteracy, disease, malnutrition, population explosion, poverty, and ignorance are on the rise.

The only way to resolve these problems is for the African national governments to engage their people in both the political process and the educational process in meaningful ways. If this is not done soon, the problems will become even more complex and the solutions still more elusive. Coups and counter coups, much in evidence in many countries of Africa today, will only serve to compound national problems. In short, the African governments must realize that the democratic process, in its genuine meaning, offers the best opportunity of solving the complex problems of national development. Zimbabwe, be well advised and be wise!

Notes

1. Ralph Dodge, "The African Church Now and in the Future," an unpublished essay, 1966. On file at the George Arents Research Library, Syracuse University.
2. J. S. Green, Rhodes Goes North (London: Bell and Son, 1936), p. 99 .
3. British South Africa Company, Records: Charles Coghlan, Ref. Co/8/1:Fols. 13-27. In the Zimbabwe National Archives.
4. T. A. O'Farrell, "Report to Annual Conference," in The Official Journal of the Methodist Church, 1928, p. 30.
5. The Report of the Kerr Commission, p. 26.
6. British South Africa Company: Records: Earl Grey, Ref. BR/1/1/11:Fols. 542-458. In the Zimbabwe National Archives.
7. Harold Jowitt, The Annual Report of the Director of Native Education, 1928, p. 15.
8. British South Africa Company Records, 1890-1900.
9. British South Africa Company, Records: Earl Grey, Report of the Administrator, 1898-1900. In the Zimbabwe National Archives.
10. Ibid.
11. Administrator of Rhodesia from December 5, 1898, to October 31, 1914. The Milton Buildings, a complex of office buildings in the center of Harare, were named after him.
12. Southern Rhodesia, The Report of the Commission of Inquiry into Native Education, L. Hadfield, Chairman, 1927, p. 15
13. J. C. Smuts, "Race Relations and Opportunity for Development in Southern Africa," address given at the banquet given in his honor by the governor-general of Mozambique, April 1, 1945. In the Zimbabwe National Archives.
14. Aldon Mwamuka, in a presidential address during an annual conference of the African Teachers Association, Mutare, July 31, 1945. In the Zimbabwe National Archives.
15. Ibid.
16. The The Report of the Kerr Commission, para. 52, p. 10.
17. Godfrey Huggins, "Taking Stock of African Education," address to the Southern Rhodesia Missionary Conference, Goromonzi, 1954.
18. Ian Smith, interview with the author, in Harare, Zimbabwe, July 20, 1983.
19. A senior teacher at George Stark Secondary School, interview with the author, at the school, August 2, 1989.

Appendices

Appendix 1

The Rudd Concession: A Colonial Deception

October 30, 1888

Know all men by these presents that whereas Charles Dunell Rudd of Kimberly, Rochfort Maguire of London, and Robert Thompson of Kimberly, hereinafter called the grantees, have covenanted and agreed, and do hereby covenant and agree to pay me, my heirs and successors the sum of one hundred pounds sterling British currency on the first day of every lunar month, and further to deliver at my Royal Kraal one thousand Martin-Henry breech-loading rifles, together with one thousand rounds of suitable cartridges, five hundred of the said rifles, and fifty thousand of the said cartridges to be ordered from England forthwith and delivered with reasonable despatch and the remainder of the said rifles and cartridges to be delivered as soon as the said grantees shall have commenced to work mining machinery within my territory and further to deliver on the Zambezi River a steamboat with guns suitable for defensive purposes upon the said river, or in lieu of the same steamboat, should I so elect, to pay me the sum of five hundred pounds sterling British currency on the execution of the presents, I, Lobengula, King of Matabeleland, Mashonaland, and other adjoining territories, in the exercise of my sovereign powers, and in the presence and with the consent of my Council of *Indunas*, do hereby grant and assign unto the said grantees, their heirs, representatives, and assigns, jointly and severally, the complete and exclusive charge over all metals and minerals situated and contained in my kingdoms principalities, and dominions, together with full power to do all things they may deem necessary to win and to procure the same, and to hold, collect and enjoy the profits and revenues, if any, derived from the said metals and minerals subject to aforesaid payment, and whereas I have been much molested of late by diverse persons seeking and desiring to obtain grants and concessions of land and mining rights in my territories, I do hereby authorize the said grantees, their heirs, representatives, and assigns, to take all necessary and lawful steps to exclude from my kingdoms, principalities, and dominations, all persons seeking land, metals, or mining rights herein, and I do hereby undertake to render them such needful assistance as they may from time to time require for the exclusion of such persons and to grant no concession of land or mining rights from or after this date without their consent and concurrence, provided that if at any time the said monthly payment of one hundred pounds shall be in arrears for a period of three months then this grant shall cease and terminate from the date of the last made payment, and further provided that nothing contained in these presents shall extend to or affect a grant made by me of certain mining rights in a portion of my territory south of the Ramokaban River, which grant is commonly known as the Tati Concession. This given under my hand this thirtieth day of October in the year of our Lord eighteen hundred and eighty -eight, at my Royal Kraal.

Lobengula, X his mark
C. D. Rudd
Rochfort Maguire
F. R. Thompson

Appendix 2

Some Highlights In The History Of Education in Zimbabwe

1859 Robert Moffat of the London Missionary Society opens the first school for Africans, at Inyati.

1870 Moffat opens the second school for Africans, at Hope Fountain.

1899 The first Education Ordinance is promulgated, providing for state financial aid to education.

1901 The first amendment to the Education Ordinance of 1899 requires African students to take industrial courses.

1908 The Hole Commission recommends safeguarding the educational interests of whites.

1911 The Graham Commission recommends that religious, industrial, and moral education form the major thrust in the education of the Africans.

1913 The Rolin Report severely criticizes the lack of adequate educational policy for Africans.

1916 The Russell Commission recommends that education for whites be made compulsory and free. This recommendation was implemented in 1935.

1920 The Keigwin Commission recommends that a small number of mission schools for Africans be developed to provide better training than is being given at the time, and that industrial and practical training form the backbone of their education.

Domboshawa training school for Africans is founded along the lines of the recommendations of the Keigwin Report.

1921 Tjolotjo training school for Africans is founded along the lines of the recommendations of the Keigwin Report.

1925 The Hadfield Commission recommends that education for Africans remain in the hands of Christian missionaries and that it remain voluntary.

The Morris Carter Land Commission recommends that the country be divided into areas for exclusive occupation by whites and Africans separately, and that education be designed to help them prepare for their respective roles in society.

1927 The Department of Native Education is established with Harold Jowitt as its director. Jowitt serves until 1934.

1928 The Tate Commission recommends that the education for whites seek to strengthen their political influence in the country.

1929 The Land Apportionment Act comes into being in accordance with the recommendation of the Morris Carter Commission of 1925.

The Hilton-Young Commission recommends the adoption of a dual system of education, one for whites and one for Africans, as had been the practice since the opening of the first school for Africans in 1859.

1935 Free and compulsory education for whites is introduced in accordance with the recommendations of the Russell Commission of 1916.

1936 The Fox Commission recommends that education should prepare different people to living and contribute to the development of, their own communities.

1939 The first secondary school for Africans is opened at St. Augustine's, near Penhalonga.

Outbreak of World War II. Africans volunteer for military service in larger numbers than they had during World War I because they are given to understand that after the war they will be given a more meaningful opportunity for development through education.

Godfrey Huggins's government (1933-1953) introduces a new educational policy for whites in order "to prevent the emergence of a poor white class."

1945 The Asquith Commission recommends that university education be considered the best means of preparing Africans, both men and women, for national service.

African leaders meet in London to plan their strategy for dealing with the problems of their life caused by the colonial condition and a response to the conclusion of the war. This meeting marks the beginning of the rise of African nationalism.

1946 The colonial government opens the first state primary school for Africans, at Chitsere in Harare, and the first secondary school, at Goromonzi.

The Beadle Commission recommends secondary education for colored students.

The British Methodist Church issues The Waddilove Manifesto which calls upon the government to formulate adequate educational policy for Africans.church organizations and the government in order to develop adequate educational policy and programs for Africans.

The Cartmel-Robinson Commission recommends that college education be available to all races on equal terms.

1953 The establishment of the Federation of Rhodesia and Nyasaland places education for whites under federal responsibility and that for African under territorial responsibility.

The Carr-Saunders Commission recommends that Africans who receive higher education eventually be allowed to seek employment opportunity under same conditions as whites.

1955 The colonial government opens the first state teacher training school for Africans in Mutare.

1956 The New Five-Year Education Plan (the Todd Plan) for Africans comes into being.

Godfrey Huggins resigns as prime minister of the Federation of Rhodesia and Nyasaland and is succeeded by Roy Welensky, highly emotional and unpredictable politician.

1957 The Bray Commission recommends that technical education be considered essential for Africans in order to ensure economic development of the country.

The University College of Rhodesia and Nyasaland is opened with 8 Africans and 60 whites.

The second state secondary school for Africans was opened at Fletcher.

1959 The African Education Act comes into being.

The Hunter Commission recommends that citizenship courses be offered to all students at the University College of Rhodesia and Nyasaland.

The Whitehead administration (1958-1962) declares a national state of emergency and arrests hundreds of African political activists, many of them teachers, causing disruption in the educational process for Africans.

1962 The Judges Commission recommends that extending equal educational opportunity to Africans be considered essential to racial peace, political stability, and development for the good of the country.

The Rhodesia Front Party is returned to power in the general elections held on December 18.

1963 The British government dissolves the Federation of Rhodesia and Nyasaland due to relentless opposition from the Africans who argue that they are denied equal opportunity in society because they are denied equal opportunity for education.

1964 Massive boycott of schools by African students leads Charles S. Davies, the secretary for African education in the Rhodesia Front government, to characterizes the year as "the year of troubles."

1965 The Rhodesia Front government (1962 — 1979) seizes political power from the governor appointed by Britain and unilaterally declares the country independent setting off the worst national crisis since the war of 1896-1897.

1966 The Rhodesia Front government announces a new educational policy for Africans entitled The Dynamic Expansion in African Education, which many observers consider neither dynamic nor an expansion.

The bitter war of independence begins with many schools, especially those in the rural areas, are closed.

1968 The Whaley Constitutional Commission recommends that education be provided for different racial groups according to the residential areas to which they will be assigned and that the Land Apportionment Act be amended to make it more effective.

1969 The Rhodesia Front government enacts the Land Tenure Act in accordance with the recommendation of the Whaley Commission, but it goes beyond the recommendation in its political action to give itself more power than is normally associated with government functions.

1970 The Rhodesia Front government forces church organizations out of the education for Africans because it wants local community organizations to assume the responsibility of running their schools.

1971 The Rhodesia Front government introduces the controversial policy of a 5 percent cut in salary grants for African primary teachers, setting off the worst crisis between the church and the government since the publication of the Rolin Report in 1913.

1972 African students begin of disappear of African students from secondary schools to join the growing number of nationalist guerrillas who are fighting to end the Rhodesia Front government.

1979 About 80 percent of the schools for Africans, especially in the rural areas, are closed because of the war.

The Lancaster House conference convenes in London to work out a new constitution for an independent Zimbabwe. Ian Smith calls it ''madness.''

1980 An independent state of Zimbabwe state of Zimbabwe announces a new educational policy providing for free and universal primary education for all students.

Appendix 3

British South Africa Company

Ordinance Number 5, July 27, 1894

Imposing and Providing for the Payment of a Hut Tax

It is hereby ordained by the British South Africa Company (hereinafter called "the Company") as follows:

1. The limits of this Ordinance shall be the parts of South Africa by the Portuguese Possessions by the South African Republic to a point opposite the mouth of the River Shashi, by the territories of the Chief Khama of the Bamangwato to the River Zambezi, and by that river to the Portuguese boundary, including an area of ten miles radius round Fort Tuli, and excluding the area of the district known as the Tati district as defined by Her Majesty's Charter dated 29th day of October, 1889.

2. From and after the periods specified in Sections 5 and 6 of this Ordinance, every male Native shall, every year pay to the Administrator of the Company or to some person in that behalf authorized by him (hereinafter called "the Collector") a Hut Tax of ten shillings in respect of the occupation of every Hut occupied by him during any part of the year. A Hut inhabited during any part of the year by any wife or by any woman of the Kraal of such Native shall, for the purpose of this Ordinance, be deemed to be occupied by him during the same period.

   Hut Tax which has accrued due shall be paid on such day and at such place as shall be appointed for the purpose by the Administrator or the Collector.

3. A payment for huts situated outside that portion of the lands within the limits of this Ordinance known as "Matabeleland" shall fall due on the last day of October, 1894, but shall be at half the above-mentioned annual rate only.

4. Any sums paid for Hut Tax by any Native before the approval of this Ordinance shall be deemed to have been paid on account, and pro tanto in discharge, of sums payable by him under this Ordinance.

5. Within the specifications made in Section Number 4 Hut Tax for a year at the full rate of 10 shillings shall fall due on the last day of July, 1895, and on 1st day of July in every succeeding year.

6. This Ordinance shall not come into force in any parts of that portion of the lands within the limits of this Ordinance known as Matabeleland until the Land Commission, constituted by Her Majesty's Order in Council of the 18th day of July, 1894, shall have made an approved settlement of the Natives on lands within such part or parts, and the Hut Tax shall be deemed to be due at the full rate mentioned in Section 2, on the 1st day of July, following the end of the year in which such settlement is made, and so on from year to year.

7. Hut Tax shall be payable in sterling coin, but in cases where the Administrator for the Collector has no alternative it may be accepted in grain or stock, the value of such grain or stock being taken to be the price current at the nearest market at which such grain or stock can be disposed of, and in all such cases the reasonable cost of carriage or driving, as the case my be, shall be paid in addition to the Hut Tax by the person tendering payment in grain or stock as aforesaid.

8. A receipt signed by the Administrator or Collector for the amount of Hut Tax paid by any person shall be delivered to him.

9. This Ordinance may be cited as The Hut Tax Ordinance, 1894.

GOD SAVE THE QUEEN

Appendix 4

Ordinance Number 18, 1899

Ordinance to provide for the appointment of Inspector of Education

Order B: Native Schools

Conditions on which aid will be granted from the public Funds to Native Mission Schools

Whereas a Native Mission School is kept for not less than four hours daily, of which not less than two hours shall be devoted to industrial training by any teacher or teachers approved of by the Administrator and the average daily attendance is not less than 50, there will be allowed annually for and in respect of each pupil who shall during the preceding year have attended the school on at least two hundred occasions the sum of ten shillings provided that in no case shall such annual allowances exceed fifty pounds.

Order C: Building Loans

Conditions on which Moneys will be advanced to certain Schools for Building Purposes

1. Undenominational Public Schools

(a) The Administrator, if satisfied upon the recommendations of the Inspector that a school is needed for the educational requirements of any locality, may, upon application for loan from the public funds on the conditions in the next succeeding clause mentioned, such amount of money not exceeding two thousand pounds as shall cover the cost of creating, on land to be provided by the British South Africa Company for the purpose, an Undenominational Public School and offices, a guarantee being furnished by the Managers of the school to the satisfaction of the Administrator that the regular payment of interest on the money so advanced will be made.

(b) The sum of money so provided and advanced shall bear interest at the rate of ten pounds per annum of which interest one-half shall be paid out of the Public Funds provided for educational purposes.

(c) After the regular payment of such interest for a period of fifteen years the principal amount shall be held to have been redeemed and the land and buildings therein shall be vested in the Municipality, if any, or Managers of the school if there is no such Municipality, to be held by them in perpetuity in trust for the inhabitants of such locality for educational purposes.

(d) Until the whole of the principal sun and interest shall have been paid in the manner aforesaid the land and buildings thereon shall be and shall remain vested in the British South Africa Company.

2. Public Voluntary Schools

(a) The Administrator, if satisfied upon the recommendation of the Inspector that a school is needed for the educational requirements of such locality and where it may appear to his satisfaction that such requirements may be more advantageously met by the establishment of a Public Voluntary School under the advance on loan from the public funds on the conditions in the next succeeding clause mentioned a sum of money not exceeding one thousand pounds towards the creation of such Public Voluntary School and offices, provided that the sum of money so advanced shall not be in excess of a similar amount to be advanced by the religious body aforesaid, a guarantee being furnished to the satisfaction of the Administrator that regular payment of interest on the amount advanced will be made.

(b) The sum of money so provided and advanced shall bear interest at the rate of ten pounds per hundred pounds per annum, of which one-half shall be paid out of the public funds provided for educational purposes. After the regular payment of such interest for a period of fifteen years the principal amount shall be held to have been redeemed.

(c) Such Public Voluntary School may be built on land either

(1) the property of the British South Africa Company, in which case the land and buildings thereon shall remain vested in the British South Africa Company until the whole of the principal and interest shall heave been redeemed in the manner aforesaid, whereon the land and buildings thereon shall become the absolute property of the religious body aforesaid,

(2) The property of the religious body aforesaid, who shall in such a case furnish to the British South Africa Company a first mortgage bond upon the whole of the land and buildings thereon, which mortgage bond shall be redeemed when the whole of the principal and interest shall have been paid in the manner aforesaid.

Order D: General

As often as any Undenominational Public School or Voluntary Public School receiving aid by way of maintenance with these Regulations shall lease any building for school purposes the Administrator may if satisfied from the report of the Inspector that the lease is necessary and that the rent is fair and reasonable, contribute from the public funds towards defraying such rent sum as he may deem fit.

Appendix 5

Ordinance Number 1, March 22, 1899

Amending the Law Relating to the Apprenticeship of Native Children

Whereas it is expedient, with a view to the establishment of technical and other schools, agricultural colleges and industrial homes for Native children in Rhodesia, to amend the law relating to apprenticeship, so as to provide for the apprenticeship of Native children to the superintendent or masters of such institutions:

Now it is hereby ordained by the British South Africa Company as follows:

(1) All and singular the provisions of the Cape Acts 15, 1856; 18, 1873; 28, 1874; 7, 1875; 8, 1889, shall *mutatis mutandis*, be deemed and taken to be applicable to the apprenticeship of Native children or Native youths to the superintendent or master of any technical school, agricultural college, model farm, industrial home or other educational institution, workshop or factory in Rhodesia.

(2) All contracts for such apprenticeship shall be executed by the parent or guardian and the superintendent or master in the presence of a Magistrate or of a Native Commissioner, and shall be drawn up as nearly as possible in terms of section 9 of Chapter III of the Cape Act 15 of 1856.

(3) This ordinance may be cited as the Apprenticeship of Native Children Ordinance Number 1, 1899.

Appendix 6

Education In Rhodesia

George Duthie, 1905

The period from 1890 to 1901 has witnessed the establishment of schools in a rather haphazard fashion by various bodies, religious and otherwise, and the gradual unification of these schools into one system by the introduction of the Education Ordinance of 1899. Schools were sometimes started where they were hardly necessary. There was a duplication of schools in some quarters which was not justified by the number of pupils, and in other cases schools which satisfied a temporary need disappeared with the migration of the population.

As the condition of the country became more settled and the population gathered into more or less populous communities, the educational needs could be more easily estimated, and a definite scheme became possible. The introduction of the Education Ordinance in 1899 crystallized matters, and in 1901 an educational system may be said to have been well established.

A distinct feature characterizes the educational advance in the subsequent fours years arising from an amendment of the Education Ordinance, which took effect in the beginning of 1903. The number of pupils per teacher is low, and is accounted for by the fact that in none of the schools is the attendance large, and, as the standards remain the same in number for almost any size of school, the staff must appear numerous and the expense per pupil correspondingly great. Six out of the thirteen schools have twenty pupils or under. Small communities are well provided for, but the problem of the outlying districts has not yet been solved, or at least only in part.

The chief machinery to teach children on farms is by boarding houses attached to schools. Of these there are six. But as the expense involved can be borne only by the wealthier parents there are still a number of children to be reached. The total number of European children between the ages of five and fifteen is 1,406. The government-aided schools account for 500 of these. These figures are a proof of the readiness of the government of Southern Rhodesia to put education within the reach of all [white] children, and in particular the high grant of over $20 per pupil is evidence of a liberality towards education which is all the more striking in the case of an administration which has not yet been able to make the revenue of the country meet expenditure. To obtain the total cost to the government of education in Southern Rhodesia, it is necessary to add to the grants the expenses of administration, which gives a total of about $15,000.

At this point nothing has been said about schools for Natives. There are about twenty-five native schools in the territory, all under the charge of missions [religious establishments] of various denominations. Only three of these are assisted by the government, which is an increase of one since 1901. The condition laid down for a government grant to native schools is that the director of education shall be satisfied that:

(1) There are at least forty pupils who have attended 150 days of four hours during the year.

(2) Industrial work is systematically taught.

(3) The pupils are taught to speak and understand the English language.

(4) The pupils are taught habits of discipline and cleanliness.

(5) The instruction is carried on in every respect in a satisfactory manner.

The reason why so few of the native schools receive government grants is either because the schools cannot comply with the necessary conditions or that the managers of the schools prefer to run their schools independently. The conditions laid down perhaps require a little explanation. In insisting on industrial [manual] education the government does not specially require training in carpentry, iron work, or such handiwork. A systematic training in household work or in agriculture is accepted. The usual forms of industrial work are domestic and agricultural work and brick making. In such a subject as agriculture it is expected that the natives understand the reasons for the various processes.

As regards teaching the native to speak and understand the English language, this does not of necessity imply the teaching of reading or writing. Teachers are encouraged to adopt the methods that have been adopted amongst white children of late years in teaching them foreign languages, that is, by word of mouth and by illustrations rather than through the medium of books. That is to say, by the method that any child naturally starts to learn its own language. Sufficient time has not yet elapsed to comment on the success or otherwise of this method, but considerable progress has been made in one instance by a method which seems to suit a certain class of natives, that is, by the rough-and-ready plan of making the pupils learn by heart a large number of English words and phrases.

It is to be remembered that in Rhodesia large numbers of natives have had very little opportunity of hearing the English language spoken, and that when they ultimately come into contact with the English-speaking inhabitants in the way of work innumerable misunderstandings arise between employer and employee. It is with a view to minimizing friction and encouraging a better relationship of mutual understanding between Europeans [whites] and Natives that so great a stress is laid on learning to speak and understanding the English language as early as possible, without the necessity on the part of the teachers of going through the laborious and often fruitless task of first teaching spelling and reading.

The teaching of habits of cleanliness is strongly insisted on, as Natives are notoriously careless in this respect. The carelessness is often a danger to the whole community. It is a subject of continual worry amongst white housekeepers to keep the Native servants from using the same water and cloths for cleaning both kitchen and bedroom utensils.

To return to the ordinance of 1903, which is the distinctive feature of the educational system during the last four years, it may be said that generally grants are offered to schools on far easier conditions than formerly. A minimum attendance of twenty-five was required under the old ordinance, but the matter of attendance is now left to the recommendation of the director and the approval of the administrator. As already stated, no fewer than six of the thirteen schools have an attendance under twenty-five, and, by the relaxation of the rule, nearly ninety children have the benefits of education which might not have been possible under the old regulation.

Formerly it was generally supposed, too, that schools should be under a board of management, but in several cases a board could not be formed. The administrator is allowed, under the new ordinance, to make such arrangements as are possible in any community where the establishment of a school is deemed advisable. This has been so liberally interpreted that at the present time the total cost of three of the schools is entirely borne by the government. In the case of only three schools does a board of management exist.

The further changes in the new ordinance deal with increased grants towards teachers' salaries, provision for boarding grants, and increased grants for extra subjects. One final word as to the range of education provided. In nearly all the schools the range is not beyond the elementary range of standard work. This is due mainly to the youth of the pupils, and in the majority of cases the teachers are capable of carrying on the work to matriculation standard. In the case of one school, St. George's School, Bulawayo, under the charge of the Jesuit Fathers, pupils are prepared, and successfully prepared, for the matriculation examination of the University of the Cape of Good Hope.

Appendix 7

Ordinance Number 133: Education Ordinance, 1907

Order D: Schools For Natives

1. Native schools of the first class are those in which there is a boarding establishment under the supervision of a European, and which can satisfy the Director that:

   (a) industrial work is systematically taught at least two hours a day during the school year,

   (b) a sufficient number of pupils are taught to speak and understand the English language,

   (c) pupils are taught habits of discipline and cleanliness,

   (d) the school hours, inclusive of the hours devoted to industrial work, shall be at least four hours a day for 180 days during the year.

   An annual grant of one pound will be given for every boarder who has attended 120 full school days during the year and made satisfactory progress

2. Second class schools for Natives are those which are under the supervision of a European teacher and provide for day scholars and satisfy the Director that:

   (a) a sufficient number of pupils are taught to speak and understand the English language,

   (b) the school is open 180 days during the year for two hours a day,

   (c) pupils are taught habits of discipline and cleanliness.

   An annual grant of ten pounds will be given in second class schools for every 20 pupils who attend 120 full school days a year and make satisfactory progress. A further annual grant of ten shillings per head will be given to those who are trained industrially for two hours a day for 120 days during the year in addition to the two ordinary school hours.

3. Third class schools for Natives are those under Native teachers where the school is open 180 days of two hours each during the year, and where pupils are taught habits of discipline and cleanliness. An annual grant of five pounds will be given for every 20 pupils who attend 120 full school days during the year and make satisfactory progress.

4. In schools where there are both boarders and day scholars a grant can be earned for boarders under the qualifications for first class schools, and for day scholars under the qualifications for second class schools.

5. An annual grant of one pound will be given for every female Native who is trained 120 days of two hours a day in domestic work and makes satisfactory progress. The domestic work must include sewing, cooking, washing, ironing and general housework.

6. Grants of half the cost will be given for the necessary equipment for the teaching of domestic work to female Natives.

7. Industrial work for Natives may include farming, brickmaking, roadmaking, building, carpentry, ironwork or domestic work as defined in Section 5. In farming each Native to earn a grant must efficiently cultivate one acre of ground.

8. The maximum grant to any Native school shall be 120 pounds per annum.

Appendix 8

Observations Of The Graham Commission On Some Aspects Of The African Culture, 1911

1. *Marriage*: Adultery and cognate acts, such as harboring, should be punishable in the case of both the man and the woman. When a parent or guardian unreasonably withholds his consent to a marriage, the Secretary for Native Affairs should have power, after due enquiry, to authorize the marriage to be registered.

2. *Lobola* [the bride price]: Thc limit of lobola fixed by law should be abrogated. We do not recommend any interference with the custom with regard to the payment of lobola. Although there are objectionable features in connection with it, there can be very little doubt that the marriage tie is looked upon as more binding where lobola has been paid, and the system unquestionably affords material benefits and protection to the female.

3. *Polygamy*: At present there is no reason to interfere with the custom of polygamy, but, owing to the objectionable incidents that are attached to it, it should be discouraged in every way. With reference to the requirements of the Churches that polygamists must discard all wives but one before admission as members, the Commission feels that, seeing that polygamy is recognized by law, there is no justification for the practice. They consider that a husband should bear the responsibility of maintaining all his wives until the marriage is properly severed by death or legal separation.

4. *Ukungena* [sexual relations outside marriage]: The Commission considers that Ukungena is one of the incidents of polygamy which will die out with it. Though recognizing the many objectionable aspects of the custom, the Commission cannot see how it can be interfered with.

5. *Pledging of Children*: The pledging of children should be punishable criminally in regard to both parties to the transaction.

6. *Girls at Mission Schools*: The admission of girls to mission stations without the consent of their parents or guardians should be prohibited.

7. *Employment of Boys*: Boys of the age of 16 and upwards should be permitted to enter into valid contracts, provided they are executed before a Magistrate or some duly prescribed official, such contracts to be binding on all parties, whether the parent or guardian consent or not.

8. *Tribal Control and Chiefs*:

   (a) That it is desirable to control the Natives as much as possible through their own Chiefs and Headmen. The power of arbitrament amongst their own people at present exercised by Chiefs should be recognized, such powers should be exercised under the control of the Native Commissioner or other District Officer.

   (b) All Chiefs should be subsidized.

   (c) The rule of succession to chieftainship in force among the Matabele should be introduced as opportunity rises throughout Southern Rhodesia. But the Administrator should have power to refuse to recognize an heir who is, in his opinion, unfit for such a position, and to appoint some other suitable person in his stead, adhering, as nearly as possible, to the prescribed rule of succession.

Appendix 9

Ordinance Number 7, July 19, 1912

To Provide For The Control of Native Schools

Be it enacted by the Administrator of Southern Rhodesia with advice and consent of the Legislative Council thereof, as follows:

1. For the purpose of this Ordinance:

   "Native" shall mean any person not of purely European descent who is a Native of South Africa or of Central Africa,

   "Manager" shall, where there is no manager, mean the principal teacher,

   "Native school" shall mean a school devoted entirely or partly to the education of Natives.

2. The manager of any Native school not subject to inspection and control as provided for in the Education Ordinance, 1903, shall within three months of the date of promulgation of this Ordinance report to the Director of Education the names and credentials of the teachers in such school, the number of pupils in attendance, the nature of the education given, and such other particulars as the said Director may from time to time require.

3. From and after the date of the promulgation of this Ordinance, no person shall open a Native school without having first received the permission of the Director of Education, who shall give his assent thereto on being satisfied as to the qualifications of the teachers whom it is proposed to employ, the nature of the subjects to be taught, and the provision to be made for the general conduct and discipline of such school, provided that it the said Director shall withhold his assent to the opening of any such school an appeal lie to the Administrator, whose decision shall be final.

4. Every Native school shall be subject to inspection by the Director of Education, or by an Inspector of Schools or other authorized officer, who shall have the right of entering such school at any time during school hours, of examining the state of the school buildings and equipment, of ascertaining the progress of the pupils, and of enquiring generally into the standing and qualifications of the teachers, the nature of the instruction given, and such other matters as may be relevant to the conduct and discipline of the school, and may call for such returns as he may require in order to obtain information on the aforesaid subjects.

5. The Director of Education may, after full enquiry, if not satisfied as to the manner in which any Native school is conducted, direct the closing of such school, or permit of its being carried on under such terms and conditions as he may direct, provided, however, that an appeal from any action taken by the Director of Education in terms of this section shall lie to the Administrator, whose decision shall be final.

6. Nothing in this Ordinance shall be taken to prevent any missionary institution from opening any Native school under an agent subject to their authority or control, provided that in such case the institution concerned shall within three months of such opening report the fact to the Director of Education, and the provision of this Ordinance shall then apply.

7. This Ordinance shall not apply to any Native school established for teaching religion only, save that the fact that such school has been opened shall be reported to the Director of Education, and any such school shall be open to inspection as herein provided, for the purpose of ascertaining whether the teaching is wholly confined to religious subjects.

8. Any person contravening the provisions of this Ordinance, or impeding or obstructing the Director of Education or Inspector of Schools or other authorized officer in carrying out the powers and duties imposed by this Ordinance, or disobeying any lawful order, shall, on conviction, be liable to a fine not exceeding 25 pounds, or in default of payment to imprisonment with or without lard labour for a period not exceeding three months.

9. This Ordinance may be cited as the Native Schools Ordinance, 1912.

Appendix 10

The Aims Of African Education, 1928

Harold Jowitt, Director of Native Education, 1927-1934

Introduction:

The first report of the newly-inaugurated Native Education Department, to be of real value, should include within its survey an accurate and detailed account of the factors involved, together with a detailed analysis of such factors leading to reasoned proposals for re-adjustment. For this purpose adequate data are essential. Such data, however, are largely absent, so that their tabulation and interpretation are to this extent rendered impossible.

The reason for this lies chiefly in the non-existence before 1928 of a Department of Native Education. Nor did there exist in Rhodesia, as in some of the other African territories, a sub-department of Native Education, which might reasonably have been expected to place on record relatively complete data regarding this work.

Until January, 1928, Native education was an appendage of the European Education Department, the step-child inevitably receiving the crumbs from the table of the accredited educational family. The growing European work, the extent of the geographical areas to be covered, the absence of any officials specially qualified in Native education, and the astounding growth of the Native schools within a generation, all tended to preclude the development of an adequate system of inspection, direction or official records which otherwise would have guided later enquiries.

Hence, it is not a matter of surprise to discover practically no data bearing upon definite conditions in over 90 per cent of the schools, upon the teaching staffs and other qualifications or duties in such schools, upon the class or age distribution of the pupils, upon their school leaving stage, upon the number of boys and girls in different parts of the educational system, upon the incidence of retardation or acceleration within the system, upon the examination system or its relation to output, upon teacher training in relation to current needs, upon the rate of increase of schools of different types or different denominations, upon educational facilities on the mines or in the towns and upon many kindred problems.

Neither is it surprising to discover incomplete data regarding the past nor in the present the existence of maladjusted curricula. Such things constitute part of the inevitable inheritance from the exigencies of a former day. Inevitably also they restrict the scope of this report. Obviously it is impossible to tabulate, collate, analyze and interpret data which are unrecorded, nor has it been possible to supply the need within the first twelve months of the new department.

In placing this fact on record there can be no question of discrediting one's predecessors. That the expanding European department with an annual budget of over a quarter of a million sterling could concurrently with its own phenomenal development so administer Native education that its liberal expansion grew apace, must always remain a signal achievement for those responsible. Their sympathy and effective support in such dual administration must for all time ensure the gratitude of those who will continue to build upon the foundations which they laid.

The Aims of Native Education:

It is not open to question that Native education in the past has suffered from a lack of clarity and general agreement regarding aims. Many who were directly responsible for educating the Natives never defined their objectives, and hence if they missed the mark it was largely because they had never set up a mark at which to aim. Those who gave definition to their aims expressed these in differing terms, and whilst having much in common, failed to reach a central unifying principle to serve in the development of criteria. This appears to have been true both of Missions and the government.

Since, however, the former have always exercised a preponderating influence over policies, and since numerically they have greatly surpassed the few government officials who have had contact with this work, the differing but largely undefined aims of the Missions have permeated the country, carrying with them their common elements, together with their lack of clarity and their educational insufficiency. It would not be difficult to show that different churches and nationalities have propounded or been influenced by inadequate and discarded aims, which by infiltration from the past service today, with a deleterious effect upon outlook and procedure.

Examples of this would be the emphasis placed upon moral or mental discipline, the distinction between liberal education for the Europeans and illiberal for the Natives, the consideration of education as the handmaid to life hereafter, or the conviction that all school work must subserve church work and be first and last pro ecclesia. To postulate this by no means signifies that a stigma should be attached to those concerned. They were walking by the light they had, and by it they walked long and faithfully. Incidentally the study of European systems, whether indigenous or transported, would reveal the acceptance of similar aims with resulting weaknesses.

The experience of the church in Rhodesia as elsewhere was that in order to stabilize the faith of converts and to assist in character development it was necessary that they should be able to read the Scriptures or other books of religious instruction translated by the missionaries. Hence was introduced the teaching of the three R's with the curricular requirement that in 88% of the schools in the country the pupils are taught to read in the Native language with elements of writing and arithmetic.

If this viewpoint were to be maintained, it would draw together two very dissimilar sections, the missionary group on the one hand, and on the other the decreasing section of the community which still regards the Native as one who should be trained by an inferior kind of education to be a better hewer of wood and drawer of water [for his white master].

Probably the best statement of the scope of aims of Native education is that laid down in the memorandum on *Educational Policy in British Tropical Africa* by the Advisory Committee, and presented by the Secretary of State for the Colonies to Parliament in March, 1925, where we read, "Education should be adapted to the mentality, aptitude, occupations and traditions of the various people, conserving as far as possible all sound and healthy elements in the fabric of their life, adapting them where necessary to changed circumstances and and progressive ideas, as an agent of natural growth and evolution. Its aim should be to render the individual more efficient in his or her condition of life, whatever it may be, and to promote the advancement of the community as a whole through the improvement of health, the training of the people in the management of their own affairs and the inculcation of true ideas of citizenship and service. It must include the raising up of capable, trustworthy, public spirited leaders of the people, belonging to their own race."

If we reduce the statement of this aim to the effective organization of experiences in socially valuable ways, we shall retain its essence. We can hardly do so without retaining our belief in the educability of the Native, the credentials of the missionary and the rich possibilities of full cooperation. With this aim we shall cease to be complacently vague. We shall strive in our system to develop the potential capacities of the Native into dynamic abilities, to plan school activities around centers of interest, to study his environment, to remember the contiguous claims of white and black, to keep in touch with what is happening elsewhere of suggestive value, to avoid institutionalizing Native life or standardizing in mechanical fashion our products, and in short, to keep the Rhodesian Native child close to the problems of his every-day life.

Whatever may be thought of Native education, there can be no quarrel with Peabody's statement that "The only remedy for an insufficient or a misdirected education is a more sensible education," and I feel convinced that the first step towards this is a restatement of aims. Between the tribal and the detribalized Natives we have to maintain racial affinities instead of creating a gulf. This aim will help us here. Where there has been disintegration of Native life, it should lead to reintegration. From this conception we should be liberated, and should envisage the larger relationships outside the walls of the school or the hours of the time table.

Appendix 11

The Aims Of African Education, 1934

George Stark, Director of Native Education, 1934-1954

Introduction:

With the close of the year the first chapter in the history of the Department of Native Education ends. Seven years ago, the department came into being, and Mr Harold Jowitt, B.A., M.Ed., was appointed director, to whom fell the task of building up the department to its present status. In November, 1934, Mr Jowitt left the Colony to take up appointment as director of education in Uganda. It is fitting here to acknowledge with gratitude the very important part which he contributed to Native development during his term of office in this country. The full significance of his work will be realized with the passing of the years. His going has been a great loss to the Colony.

The year 1934 has been one of tenseness due to an uncertainty which the Missions have felt regarding the future of Native education. This uneasiness found expression at the Missionary Conference held at Zimbabwe in June and in December at the meeting of the advisory board for Native development. Various factors contributed to this sense of of insecurity. The Missions regarded the introduction of a new quota system to grants-in-aid as a retrograde move which would affect adversely the finances of the Missions. The resignation of Mr. Jowitt was a second contributory cause of the uneasiness in the Mission field. They felt that the person who had guided the department from its inauguration could ill afford to be spared.

The rumor set to work with such effect that the Prime Minister Godfrey Huggins, [1933-1952] considered it expedient to assure the missionary representatives of the meetings of the advisory board for Native development that it was not the intention of the government to discontinue the policy adopted in previous years for Native education, but merely to bring about a change in the method of administration.

The Aims of Native Education:

Steady improvement is being effected in the training given to the future teachers of the village schools. The raising of entrance qualifications from Standard II to Standard IV for Native teachers' courses is a step in the right direction and the aim of this department, though it is recognized that to have passed Standard IV is very meagre qualification for admission to a teacher training course. So it is the intention of the department gradually to raise the entrance qualifications to Standard VI.

Of all the different classes of Native schools in the territory the training school is the one in which the most advanced instruction is given. Consequently there is the danger that such training may become isolated from actual village conditions. The teachers should be trained not in adapting themselves to life on a mission station which is not their home, but in the improvement of the actual conditions in the reserve from which they have come and to which they will return, the chief medium for such improvement being the village school in which they will teach.

To attain this result a training in the three R's would be valueless, and hence, the curriculum of the training school is to be so adjusted that it will also include training which is specially adapted to reserve conditions. An essential part of every teacher's training is community work. Where the training school is situated on or near a Native reserve it has been a fairly easy matter, with the cooperation of the native commissioner, to give effective training.

In the industrial training of teachers particularly, the utmost care must be exercised to ensure that the training given will bring about the greatest efficiency of teachers in the conditions with which they will be faced on their return to the village school. Therefore the fundamental objective in Native education must be to make an effort to bind more closely the ties between the school and tribal life. If the foundations of Native education are to be well laid, there must be an emphasis placed upon the village school system. True education does not come from books, but passes from person to person. The efficacy of the teacher depends on what he is, rather than upon what he knows. This is why this department emphasizes character training for Native children in this Colony.

Powerful as it is, education is a dangerous instrument in the hands of those who, because of their anti-social tendencies, use it for purposes contrary to the welfare of any group of people whose traditions differ fundamentally from those of the European race which determines the course of civilization. For Natives, the school requires constant, painstaking and systematic directive supervision.

The underlying principles which govern the course of Native education, reading and writing, do not matter until the material basis of living has been assured. In no profession is the fortune of the individual's work, however humble his lot, more dependent upon his own skills and adjustment. The most enlightened propaganda must fail if it is disseminated among primitive people still in the grip of superstition, ignorance, and age-old custom. Character is the most important to the development of the Native in his emergence from barbarism. Education for the Native must seek to equip him to deal with his environment and fit him to live in his condition.

It is a truism to say that education cannot be imposed on a people. If a people remain adamant to all teaching, it is impossible for any progress to be made. If the people themselves can be aroused to take a deep interest in their own development half the battle is won. By emphasizing the social aspect of education and by adjusting the curricula of the schools so as to give this social bias to the activities of all pupils, be they in the advanced training schools or in the rudimentary village schools, this Department has sought to obviate the danger of producing a pupil who would be out of touch with his own people.

An education in the three R's only has been consistently condemned by this Department. Rather, it has been sought to emphasize a training in head, heart, and hand, and so produce a good citizen. These have been the aims and ideals of this Department.

Appendix 12

The Aims of Education

The Education Committee, 1943

Schools of every type must endeavor to fulfill their purpose in so far as they foster the free growth of individuality, helping every boy and girl to achieve the highest degree of individual development of which he or she is capable in and through the life of a society. The national tradition must be the basis of an effective education.

In this regard, education today is primarily regarded in terms of growth of soul, mind, and body. It is exploratory and creative rather than mere passive receptivity to information selected for the child by his elders. The blighting effects of education for instruction are well depicted by William Wordsworth in the lines:

Heaven lies about us in our infancy.
Shades of the prison-house begin to close
Upon the growing boy,
But he beholds the light, and whence it flows
He sees it in his joy.

Today schools must endeavor to broaden their aims, and must endeavor to teach children how to live, how to retain their ideals, their perception of the light, and whence it flows, and their joy in beholding it, endeavoring, moreover, to abolish the onset of dull disillusionment as manhood succeeds youth.

Philosophy and intellectual attitude are high-sounding terms, yet their rudiments are within the powers of any pupil to find school work interesting, to see the difference between fact and fiction, and to acquire an outlook, a habit of mind, a sense of values, an insight into the science of good and evil. This will later ripen into a rational conviction. The fundamental aim of education is to put into the mind some idea of what these things are, some desire to pursue them. An education that does this is a success, and an education that does less is a failure.

A man's peace of mind, his integrity, his sense of responsibility and consequently his values as a citizen depend on his having a standard of conduct which he understands and which satisfies his sense of rightness and justice. In a totalitarian state he is not encouraged or even allowed to judge these matters for himself. The controlling authority lays down the standard and from him is required blind obedience and blind loyalty. The burden of moral responsibility is removed from his shoulders, whether or not he wishes to carry that burden. The aim of education is to enable him to understand and accept that responsibility.

The period of conscious training with this end in view ends for many when they leave school. It is essential, therefore, that the schools should understand their responsibility and work in the closest possible cooperation with the other great formative influences, notably the home and the church. Obviously when a child first goes to school he is in no way able to judge his conduct for himself. As his understanding expands, he becomes increasingly fitted to have placed on his shoulders a greater degree of the responsibility for directing his own powers. It is the aim of education to enable him to discharge this solemn responsibility.

During the recent debate in the House of Commons on the Education Bill one member spoke of the people who know the price of everything and the value of nothing. Such people are the natural and inevitable product of any system of education that fails to find the time to interest and guide its pupils in the exercise of their judgment.

There are two fundamental *desiderata* in the art of helping children to develop an inner feeling of respect and reverence for what is fine and grand. The first is a proper choice of subject matter and its method of presentation. The second is the development of the personality of the people who are regarded by the children as being in a position of authority, out of school as well as in school. The ordinary curriculum must abound in opportunity, providing the pressure of examinations leaves time for a genuine examination of motives.

Children of different ages and races live in a world which is rightly and naturally very different from the world of adults. It is important that those who handle them should both be able to select those aspects of a story that the children are capable of understanding and applying in their own world, and be capable, too, of presenting the story as to equals. It is so easy to talk above their heads and to talk down to them. Both faults render the speaker not only futile but even dangerous to the children's moral and spiritual development.

The importance of the personality of the teacher cannot be overemphasized. The teaching profession has no place for prigs. A teacher, like other folk, should be human, and it is most necessary that he, of all people, should lay no claim to infallibility. He needs to have his head in or near the clouds, but his feet must be firmly planted on the ground. Life, in and out of school, is a matter of hard facts with plenty of gleams of sunshine, and children of all ages and races need to face facts fearlessly. Adult standards of judgment for juvenile offences — the rule of fear — engender cynicism, and "the end justifies the means" attitude, and anti-social outlook. The other extreme, kindly "soppiness" in dealing with children, leads to a romantic sentimentality which renders the unfortunate victim quite unable to face up to difficulties.

Perhaps the greatest handicap under which men and women of our generation suffer is our disinclination to attempt anything outside our vocation unless we believe that we are likely to shine at it. For, if we succeed less well than others, particularly if the others are in an inferior social or economic station, we feel humiliated and fear to lose caste. The result is that the success of another seems to detract from our own self-esteem, and we are more apt to emphasize faults, even minor faults, than to give credit where credit is due.

It is not easy to overcome this form of disability, even if we realize it. But the school can do much to prevent its emergence. As long as we, as teachers and parents, put children against each other, and lead them to believe that they are superior personalities because they come high up in form order, or inferior, as the case may be, so long shall we be guilty of warping their full development and of training misfits for society. Any school that fails to uphold this basic principle fails in seeking the fulfillment of one of its basic aims of education.

It is for this reason that every school must endeavor some basic aims: (a) to help children proceed as far along the path of attainment as they are able. (b) to help each student first to discover inherent abilities and interests and then to develop them. (c) to help him see his world, not in terms of race, but in terms of the meaning of universal values which make all people, regardless of their race, equal in society. (d) to develop dependable citizens who take pride in simple work well done, providing each child is given the kind of education from which he can benefit so that his society can benefit from it in return. (e) to help every student acquire basic skills in thinking independently and in logical manner in his interaction with people who are different from himself.

In short the aim of education should be to combat illiteracy, to lay the foundations of culture by arousing interest in the attributes of truth, goodness and beauty, to awaken a sensitivity to, and tolerance of, diversity as an enrichment of society, to help children think of education for life as something far more important than the subjects taught in school, and to help them grow into an adult society as individuals prepared to play their role in seeking its improvement. These are the aims of education anywhere, they are the aims of education in Southern Rhodesia as this committees sees them.

Appendix 13

The Waddilove Manifesto:

The Education Policy Of The [British] Methodist Church

February 9, 1946

We affirm that education is the dual responsibility of both the Church and the State, each having its own sphere of duty and of privileges. The State has been accorded power and authority to control the material and technical resources necessary for the nation's welfare.

It is the function of the Church to train and inspire teachers who have a vocation for the education of youth, and by its contact with the life of the school, help to create an atmosphere in which the hearts of youth will turn naturally towards God.

We believe that legislative safeguards should assure to Christian teaching a fundamental place in all schools, except in those specially provided for children of non-Christian faiths.

In pursuance of our Divine Purpose we affirm that the Methodist Church welcomes every opportunity to participate in African education. We remain convinced that in doing so we are fulfilling the part of our missionary calling, believing, as we do, that in the acquisition of knowledge a Christian can validly fulfill the aim of sound education inspired by Christian purpose.

We believe that the cooperation of the government in the Methodist schools is compatible with our missionary purpose, provided that no restrictions are enforced which prevent or hinder the exercise of our Divine Mission.

We believe that public money should be made available to the Church for purposes of educational function, and that the grants should be commensurate with the standards adopted by the government.

While recognizing the government responsibility for the education of its people, we declare the right of the Church with or without government assistance to offer education to all who desire it.

We assert that the Christian purpose of our educational work can only be achieved by the employment of Christian teachers in our schools. The employment of teachers who cannot enter fully into the life of the Church, whose lives do not witness to the Truth which it is our purpose to preach, is contrary to our purpose.

We believe that a satisfactory educational policy awaits a clearer enunciation of principles regarding the African's place in social, economic, and political life of the country. The formation of definite lines of development by the Africans is essential so that they reach the full and unrestricted citizenship which we believe is unquestionably their right.

Provision for higher education should be made, not in the interest of the few who may be fortunate enough to receive it, but in the interest of the general advancement of the African people as a whole.

Appendix 14

Taking Stock Of African Education

An address to the Southern Rhodesia Missionary Conference held at Goromonzi

Godfrey Huggins

August 25, 1954

After the efforts of Missionaries and Government over the last sixty years or seventy years to raise the Africans from their primitive state we ought to take stock of the position and see where our efforts are leading us.

It is usually true to say that the more primitive the African, the easier is the problem both to administer and to educate. You have impressionable material. You can deal with basic matters without having to consider complications which are eventually caused when the primitive man becomes, to a certain extent, sophisticated.

In this country we have got beyond the primitive stage and we have now to deal with the very much more complicated problems of the African who has absorbed Western ways in certain directions and is to a greater or lesser extent sophisticated. In surveying the problems which arise at this stage we need to look not only at this country hut at Africa south of the Sahara.

In trying to uplift the African we are really trying to change his environment. It is probably true that if there are any fundamental differences of mental make up between the Africans and Europeans which are the result of heredity, these are so slight as to be not demonstrable. This means that we are attempting to change not the African but the influence which operate on the African since birth and which produce those vast and profound differences which do undoubtedly exist between Africans and Europeans.

Carruthers, in his illuminating report on the psychology of the Mau Mau, classifies the environment factors which account for the observed diversities as climate, infective, nutritional and cultural. The last is, of course, the most vital.

The task of changing the environment of the African in these four connections is a stupendous one when one considers their numbers and the great changes that have to be made. But it is by no means an impossible task and we can derive great hope from this. The doctrine of segregation is based in the belief that there are certain fundamental unchangeable differences between the races and that these differences can never be reconciled. If one concedes that the differences are environmental then it follows that the differences can, over a period of time, be reconciled.

Education for the African is but a small part of this cultural background and our attempts to educate him have produced results not altogether encouraging. All too often the education of the African has opened his eyes to Western civilization and caused him to think that the little learning he possesses is the key to European culture and civilization and its consequent power.

In 1934 I wrote an article for Eastern Africa Today and Tomorrow in which I stated, "There are earnest people who believe that the shorter catechism, the multiplication table, and possibly a pair of braces, are the only steps between barbarism and civilization. Civilization acquired by such means is a hot house product and quickly dies if left to its own devices." Twenty years later the only amendment to this I would make would be to alter the list to read "the shorter catechism, the multiplication table, a pair of braces and possibly a pair of sun glasses."

The exaggerated importance attached to this little learning has led to the rise of African nationalism based on the belief that a small number of Africans, with a limited amount of learning, can govern a country without the presence of any Europeans.

We have only a small number of Africans with anything like a European standard of education, but modesty does not rank amongst their most pronounced characteristics. Because they are outstanding amongst their own people, they automatically assume that they are outstanding when compared with Europeans. They fail to realize their limitations and do not appreciate that the education which they have received is but a tiny fraction of the sum total of Western culture and civilization as we know it.

We see so many semi-educated Africans in the vanguard of nationalist movements. Even if they may appreciate what a slow process is the elevation of the African and even though they may realize what great strides are being made, they are none the less impatient. They are not content to realize that the next generation of Africans may be better off in all ways. They want quick results for themselves and they see an opportunity to acquire power while the gulf between them and their more primitive fellow beings is wide.

This same phenomenon has occurred in other territories in Africa and has provided a very powerful nationalist force. In certain territories where there had been no European settlement, the governing power had the alternative of quashing the nationalist movement or getting out. The alternative chosen was to retire from the scene and to do this they were obligated to hurry on the process of self-government, irrespective of whether the indigenous inhabitants were fit for it.

In this country, conditions are different, but we have the sad spectacle of so many of our so-called educated Africans frittering away their entire energies on some completely unattainable objective such as self-government for one part or another of the Federation [of Rhodesia and Nyasaland, 1953-1963].

This situation presents two problems for the Government and those concerned with the uplift of the African. The first is how to deal with the immediate situation caused by the misguided so-called African intellectuals. This situation can only be dealt with by firmness by making it clear that the Government will in no circumstances tolerate active or passive disobedience to any law and that their aims are completely beyond the bounds of realization. We can only hope that they do not try to test their strength because on this point we have to be quite firm.

The second problem is how to develop the African so that the educated ones do not waste their time in sterile and futile nationalistic agitation but play their full part within the existing political and economic framework of the country so as to contribute to the well-being of their own people and the nation to the maximum possible extent. There is no doubt that we have a number of Africans who do appreciate facts and play their part in this way. Their contribution to this country is very considerable. It is these people who are going to be true civilized Africans, who are going to lead their people into the promised land.

It is up to us to encourage the growth of these people in mental stature and in numbers by all the means in our power.

One objective of educating the Africans is to create a sufficiently large stratum of sensible and civilized Africans from amongst whose ranks wise leadership can be found. But side by side with education must go a concentration on other qualities which go towards making up the cultural background of the emergent African. The limitations to education without the correct background of moral and spiritual values must be realized. We must encourage the development of moral courage.

The African with one foot in his primitive cultural background is very susceptible to intimidation both psychological and physical, and civilized Africans must learn to stand out against the mob.

As regards physical intimidation we must demonstrate that the Government will always protect them. Honesty and integrity in positions of responsibility are not lightly acquired by people whose earlier traditions were based on different standards although equally moral according to their own lights. It must be realized that bribery and corruption make democratic government impossible and yet this is going to be one of the most difficult traits to remove from the African.

The reason for this is the custom of centuries of tribal life where the giving of presents to obtain favours was quite a normal procedure and the greater the favour required, the larger the present. It is one of the problems which is giving the Prime Minister of the Gold Coast [Kwame Nkrumah] a considerable headache. He himself seems to be a very exceptional African and quite above the old tribal habits; his integrity has never been challenged.

But above all must be learnt that tolerance of the other person's point of view which the Western world has only imperfectly acquired over the last two hundred years.

Of course, the European is no less influenced by his environment. People here get very upset at certain expressions of public opinion in Britain concerning affairs in Africa. This is only because the people in England live in a different environment from the one out here. The people there are basically no different.

Even out here the environment is not static but constantly changing. The environment of this country 30 or 40 years ago is vastly different from what it is today and mainly because of the way the African has advanced.

The European has got to obey the laws of nature and adapt himself to a changing environment. It is a basic biological rule that creatures which fail to adapt themselves to their environment perish. So many of our people, particularly those who have been here for along time, cannot bring themselves to realize that circumstances have changed vastly and will continue to change. It is this that causes them to express unnecessary fears about the future welfare of their children.

They fail to appreciate that their children will be infinitely better fitted to deal with future circumstances than they themselves are. Kicking against the pricks will get them nowhere. There is always the chance that when their children become adults they will be out-of-date, fossilized and a menace to their own children's future.

Bibliography

Books

Andrews, F.C. *John White of Mashonaland.* New York: Negro Universities Press, 1935.

Atkinson, Norman, *Teaching Rhodesians: A History of Educational Policy in Rhodesia.* London: Longman, 1972.

Austin, Reginald. *Racism and Apartheid in Southern Rhodesia.* Paris: Unesco, 1975.

Banana, C. S. *Theology of Promise: The Dynamics of Self-reliance.* Harare: The College Press, 1982.

Bigelow, F. *White Man's Africa.* London: Harper & Brothers, 1898.

Boggie, J. M. *First Steps in Civilizing Rhodesia.* Bulawayo: Belmont Press, 1940.

Bull, Theodore. *Rhodesia: Crisis of Color.* Chicago: Quadrangle Books, 1967.

Carter, Gwendolyn, and Patrick O'Meara. *Southern Africa: The Continuing Crisis.* Bloomington: Indiana University Press, 1978.

Chambliss, J. E. *The Life and Labors of David Livingstone.* Westport, Conn.: Negro Universities Press, 1875.

Cox, Courtland. *African Liberation.* New York: Black Education Press, 1972.

Curle, Adam. *Education for Liberation.* New York: John Wiley and Sons, 1972.

Dacks, A. J. *Christianity South of the Zambezi.* Gweru: Mambo Press, 1973.

Davis, A. *The Native Problem in South Africa.* London: Chapman and Hall, 1902.

Diffendorfer, Ralph (ed.). *The World Service of the Methodist Episcopal Church.* Chicago: Council of the World Board of Benevolences, 1928.

Dodge, Ralph E. *The Unpopular Missionary.* Westwood N. J. : Fleming H. Revell, 1964.

Fraser, D. *The Future of Africa.* Westport, Conn.: Negro Universities Press, 1911.

Gray, Richard. *The Two Nations: Aspects of Development of Race Relations in the Rhodesia and Nyasaland.* London: Oxford University Press, 1960.

Green, J. S. *Rhodes Goes North.* London: Bell and Sons, 1936.

Holeman, F. C. *Chief, Council and Commissioner: Some Problems of Government in Rhodesia.* Assen, Netherlands: Van Garcun, 1969.

Hopgood, David. *Africa in Today's World Focus.* New York: Ginn and Company, 1971.

Kapenzi, Geoffrey. *A Clash of Cultures: Christian Missionaries and the Shona of Rhodesia.* Washington, D.C.: University Press of America, 1978.

Knorr, K. *British Colonial Theories.* Toronto: University of Toronto Press, 1974.

Lyons, Charles. *To Wash and Aethiop White: British Ideas About Black African Educability, 1530-1960.* New York: Teachers College Press, 1975.

Mazikana, P. C., and I. J. Johnston. *Zimbabwe Epic.* Harare: Zimbabwe National Archives, 1982.

Memmi, Albert. *The Colonizer and the Colonized.* Boston: Beacon Press, 1965.

Monk, William (ed.). *Dr. Livingstone's Cambridge Lectures.* London: Bell and Daldy, 1860.

Mugomba, Agrippah, and Mougo Nyaggah. *Independence Without Freedom: The Political Economy of Colonial Education in Southern Africa.* Santa Barbara, Calif.: ABC-Clio, Inc., 1980.

Mungazi, Dickson. *Education and Government Control in Zimbabwe: A Study of the Commissions of Inquiry, 1908-1974.* New York: Praeger , 1990.

Mungazi, Dickson. *The Struggle for Social Change in Southern Africa: Visions of Liberty.* New York: Taylor and Francis, 1989.

Mungazi, Dickson. *To Honor the Sacred Trust of Civilization: History, Politics, and Education in Southern Africa.* Cambridge, Mass.: Schenkman Publishers, 1983.

Mungazi, Dickson. *The Underdevelopment of African Education: A Black Zimbabwean Perspective.* Washington, D.C.: University Press of America, 1982.

Mungazi, Dickson. *The Cross Between Rhodesia and Zimbabwe: Racial Conflict in Rhodesia, 1962-1979.* New York: Vantage Press, 1981.

Nyangani, Wellington. *African Nationalism in Zimbabwe.* Washington, D.C.: University Press of America, 1978.

Parker, Franklin. *African Development and Education in Southern Rhodesia.* Columbus, Ohio: Kappa Delta Pi, 1960.

Peck, A. J. *Rhodesia Accuses.* Boston: Western Islands Press, 1966.

Samkange, Stanlake. *What Rhodes Really Said About Africans.* Harare: Harare Publishing House, 1982.

Samkange, Stanlake. *Origins of Rhodesia.* New York: Frederick Praeger, 1968.

Sithole, Ndabaningi. *African Nationalism.* London: Oxford University Press, 1968.

Taylor, R. *African Education in Rhodesia.* Salisbury: Government Printer, 1970.

Tichawapedza, Fungai. *Zimbabwe Woman.* Washington, D.C.: ZANU Information Office, 1978.

Williams, G. Mennen. *Africa for the Africans.* Grand Rapids, Mich.: Eerdmans, 1969.

Willis, A. J. *An Introduction to the History of Central Africa.* London: Oxford University Press, 1964.

Wilmer, E. T. (ed.). *Zimbabwe Now.* London: Rex Collins, 1973.

Archival Materials

Ordinances

Ordinance Number 5: Imposing the Payment of Native Taxes, 1894.

Orders in Council. 1894: Section 18

Ordinance Number 6: Providing for the Prevention of Theft of Stock. 1899.

Ordinance Number 2: Native Marriages. 1901

Ordinance Number 8: The Appointment of the Inspector of Education, 1899.

Ordinance Number 269: Education Ordinance. 1902.

Ordinance Number 1: Education Ordinance, 1903.

Ordinance Number 133: Education Ordinance. 1907.

Ordinance Number 7: Control of Native Schools. 1912.

Commissions of Inquiry into Education

Commission of Inquiry into Education, Marshall Hole, Chairman, Ref. A/5/08, 1908.

Commission of Inquiry into Native Affairs, James Graham, Chairman, Ref. NA/10/11. 1911.

Commission of Inquiry into White Education, Alexander Russell, Chairman, Ref. A/2/17. 1917.

Commission of Inquiry into Industrial Development of Natives Herbert Keigwin, Chairman, Ref. A/7/20. 1920.

The Report of the Land Commission, Morris Carter, Chairman, Ref. CSR/3/26, 1925.

Commission of Inquiry into Native Education, F. L. Hadfield, Chairman, Ref. NE/3. 1927.

Commission of Inquiry into Education in East and Southern Africa, E. Hilton-Young, Chairman, Ref. EESA/3. 1928.

Commission of Inquiry into Native Education, B. H. Barnes,Chairman, Ref. NE/2. 1929.

Commission of Inquiry into Education, Frank Tate, Chairman, Ref. CSR/27/L4604, 1929.

Commission of Inquiry into Education [H.B. Fox, Chairman] Ref. CSR/25/2264, 1936.

British Colonial Office. Report of the Commission on Higher Education in the Colonies, Justice Asquith, Chairman, Ref. Cmd. 6647. 1945.

Commission of Inquiry into the Education of Coloreds, Hugh Beadle, Chairman, Ref. No/26. 1946.

The Report of the Commission of Inquiry into Native Education, Alexander Kerr, Chairman. 1951.

The Report of the Commission of Inquiry into Higher Education in the Central African Territories, Harold Cartmel-Robinson, Chairman. 1951.

Central African Council, The Report of the Commission on Higher Education for Africans in Central Africa, Alexander M. Carr-Saunders, Chairman. 1953.

The Federation of Rhodesia and Nyasaland. "The Report of the Survey of Facilities for Technical Education in the Federation, F. Bray, Chairman, Ref. C/Fed/88-GP/1523-450/24/4/58. 1958.

Association for Colleges of Citizenship. The Report of the Commission on Colleges of Citizenship in the Federation of Rhodesia and Nyasaland and Kenya. B.A. Fletcher and C.M. Capon, Co-Chairmen. 1959.

The Report of the Commission of Inquiry into Discontent in the Mangwende Reserve, James Brown, Chairman. 1961.

The Report of the Commission of Inquiry into Native Education V.A. Judges, Chairman. 1962.

Official Memos and Documents

Southern Rhodesia. *Legislative Debates.* 1896-1923.

British Colonial and Imperial Office. The Constitution for Southern Rhodesia Conferring Responsible Government. Section 28, 1923.

British South Africa Company. Information for intending settlers in Southern Rhodesia. 1901.

Rhodes, Cecil John. Memorandum to the British South Africa Company. File Ms/L0/1/1/9. April 15, 1899.

British South Africa Company. Information for Intending Settlers in Southern Rhodesia. 1901.

Chief Native Commissioner for Mashonaland. Annual Report. 1901-1916.

Chief Native Commissioner for Matabeleland. Annual Report. 1901-1915

Duthie, George. Report of Inspection Visit of St. Augustine's School for Natives. November 1901.

British South Africa Company, Reports on the Administration, Ref.S/BR-711. 1889-1902 (Two Reports).

Milton, William. Government Notice Number 277 (the Naming of the Graham Commission). July 5, 1910.

Beit Trust. Statement of the Operations of the Trust from the Date of Operation to December 31, 1913.

British South Africa Company. Records: Charles Coghlan [Premier from October 1, 1923, to September 1, 1927]: Co/8/: Folios 13-27.

British Colonial Office and Imperial Office. The Constitution for Southern Rhodesia. 1923. Section 28.

Southern Rhodesia. Parliamentary Debates. 1924-1954.

Jowitt, Harold. Annual Report of the Director of Native Education. 1927-1934.

Southern Rhodesia. Report of the Director of Native Development. 1927-1935.

Southern Rhodesia. Government Notice Number 676/29. 1929.

Southern Rhodesia. Annual Report of the Chief Native Commissioner. 1934-1954.

Stark, George. Annual Report of the Director of Native Education. 1934-1954.

Southern Rhodesia. Government Notice Number 277/35. 1935.

Southern Rhodesia. Education Act. 1938.

Huggins, Godfrey. Education Policy in Southern Rhodesia: Notes on Certain Aspects. 1939.

Huggins, Godfrey. ''Rhodesia Leads the Way: Education for Europeans in Southern Rhodesia.'' In Times Educational Supplement, February 14, 1931.

Southern Rhodesia. Government Notice Number 358/39. 1939.

Southern Rhodesia. Native Councils Act, as amended 1943.

Davies, Charles S. Letter to superintendent of instruction at Old Mutare, discussing the opening of a Methodist secondary school for Africans. September 8, 1949.

Native Commissioner for Mangwende Reserve. Memo to the Head Office, Department of Native Affairs. Ref. 191/79. 1950.

Federation of Rhodesia and Nyasaland. Report on Education for the Year 1953-1954.

Todd, Garfield. New Five-Year Education Plan for Natives. 1956.

Morris, S. C. ''Chief Mangwende Is Deposed and Banished,'' statement of reasons. January 14, 1960.

British South Africa Company Records: Earl Grey, [Administrator from April 2, 1896 to December 4, 1898]: GR/1/1/11: Folios 547-458.

Articles

Duthie, George, Inspector of Schools, ''Report of the Inspection Visit of St. Augustine's School for Natives,'' November, 1901.

Duthie, George, ''Education in Rhodesia,'' in *The British South Africa Association for the Advancement of Science,* Vol. 4, 1905, pp. 321-24.

McIntosh, R. ''Education of Children of Farmers in Southern Rhodesia.'' In *Rhodesia Agricultural Journal.* Vol. 22, 1925, pp. 290-26.

Milton, William [Administrator from December 5, 1898 to December 31, 1914]: Government Notice Number 177, the naming of the Graham Commission, a letter dated July 5, and July 14, 1910.

Mungazi, Dickson A. ''Strategy for Power: Commissions of Inquiry into Education and Government Control in Colonial Zimbabwe.'' In *The International Journal of African Historical Studies* (Boston University), Vol. 22, No. 2, 1989.

Mungazi, Dickson A. ''To Bind Ties Between the School and Tribal Life: The Educational Policy for Africans Under George Stark in Zimbabwe.'' In *The Journal of Negro Education* (Howard University), Vol. 58, No. 2, 1989.

Mungazi, Dickson A. ''Cultures in Collision: Education and Dialogical Encounter on Zimbabwe.'' In *Educational Management* (University of Oregon), January, 1987.(Microfiche.)

Mungazi, Dickson A. ''The Educational Policy of the British South Africa Company Towards Rural and Urban Africans in Zimbabwe: A Dilemma of Choice.'' In *The African Urban Quarterly* (State University of New York, Albany), Vol. 2, No. 1, 1987.

Mungazi, Dickson A. ''Application of Memmi's Theory of the Colonizer and the Colonized to the Conflicts in Zimbabwe.'' In *The Journal of Negro Education* (Howard University), Vol. 54, No. 4, Fall 1986.

Mungazi, Dickson A. ''Educational Innovation in Zimbabwe: Possibilities and Problems.'' In *The Journal of Negro Education* (Howard University), Vol. 54, No. 2, Spring 1985.

Mungazi, Dickson A. ''The Educational Policy for Africans and Church-State Conflict During the Rhodesia Front Government in Zimbabwe.'' In *National Social Science Journal* (Gannon University), Vol. 2, No. 3, 1990.

Todd, Garfield. ''A Plea for Better Education for Natives.'' In *The African Weekly,* Vol. 3, No. 2, June 12, 1946.

Miscellaneous Items

Baker-Jones, E. ''Survey of Dictionaries in School Boarding Hostels in Southern Rhodesia.'' Salisbury: Department of Education, 1941.

Challiss, Robert. ''The Educational Policy of the British South Africa Company in Southern Rhodesia, 1899-1904.'' Master's thesis, University of Cape Town, 1968.

Dodge, Ralph E. ''The African Church Now and in the Future.'' George Arents Research Library, Syracuse University, 1966. (Unpublished essay.)

Grant, Kennedy. ''Teach the Children the Art of Living Together.'' Address to the Conference of African Teachers, Harare, September 16, 1947.

Grove, G. C. ''The Planting of Christianity in Africa.'' London: SPCK, 1959.

Southern Rhodesia Missionary Conference, Goromonzi, August 26, 1954.

Huggins, Godfrey. ''Partnership in Building a Country.'' Campaign speech, December 21, 1950.

Huggins, Godfrey. ''Partnership in Rhodesia and Nyasaland.'' Speech given during a campaign for the establishment of the Federation of Rhodesia and Nyasaland, May, 1950.

Huggins, ''Taking Stock of African Education.'' Address to the Southern Rhodesia Christian Conference. Goromonzi, August 25, 1954.

Jowitt, Harold, ''The Reconstruction of African Education in Southern Rhodesia.'' Master's thesis, University of Cape Town, 1927.

Keigwin, Herbert. Letter to chief native commissioner. December 8, 1919.

Livingstone, David. ''Missionary Travels in Southern Africa: 1857-1870.'' London: SPCK, 1870.

Lloyd, B. W. ''The Early History of Domboshawa School, 1920-1939.'' Ref. MS/AFs/7499. London: Rhodes House.

MacHarg, James. ''Influences Contributing to the Education and Culture of Native People in Southern Rhodesia.'' Ph.D. dissertation, Duke University, 1962.

MacKenzie, Norman, ''The Outlook in Central Africa.'' Inaugural address delivered at the University College of Rhodesia and Nyasaland, August 7, 1959.

Macmillan, Harold. ''Commonwealth Independence and Interdependence.'' Address to joint session of the South African Parliament, Cape Town, February 3, 1960.

Makweche, D. D. ''An Account of the History of the Knight-Bruce College for Africans at St. Augustine's Mission, Penhalonga,'' Essay. N.D. (Copy sent to author by the principal of St. Augustine's School, 1966.)

Methodist Church. ''The Waddilove Manifesto: The Education Policy of the Methodist Church.'' A statement of principles and objectives. February 8-9, 1946.

Methodist Church. *Official Journal of the Methodist Church.* 1901-1954.

Methodist Episcopal Church. ''Africa Today'' in *The Africa Christian Advance,* Vol. 2, No. 1, 1918.

Mungazi, Dickson A. ''The Change of Black Attitudes Towards Education in Rhodesia, 1900-1975.'' Ph.D. dissertation, University of Nebraska, Lincoln, 1977.

National Council of Churches. ''Africa is Here.'' New York: Board of Foreign Missions, 1952.

Rolin, Henri. *Les Lois et l'Administration de la Rhodesie.* Bruxelles: Etablissement Emil Bruyant, 1913.

Royal Charter of the Founding of the University College of Rhodesia and Nyasaland. February 10, 1955. Article 4.

Smuts, J. C. "Race Relations and Opportunity for Development in Southern Africa." Address at the banquet given in his honor by the governor-general of Mozambique, August 1, 1945.

South African Ministry of Information. "South Africa Stops Native Students from Territories Outside Its Borders from Attending Its Schools." November 2, 1950 (press release.)

Southern Rhodesia Farmers Conference. Resolution on Education. Issued following a conference at Gweru, March, 1916.

Todd, Garfield, "African Education in Southern Rhodesia: The Need for a Commission of Inquiry." address to the Bulawayo National Affairs Association, February 18, 1947.

University College of Rhodesia and Nyasaland, Department of Education. The Less Successful Secondary School Child. Occasional Paper No. 1, August, 1962.

Periodicals and Newspapers

The African Weekly. 1945-1954.

The Bantu Mirror, 1946-1953.

The Rhodesia Herald. August 24, 1902; January 31, 1903; April 4, 1903, September 7, 1917;

The Daily News, 1958-1962.

Umbowo, 1946-1973.

Personal Interviews

Dangarembga, Amon, former principal, Old Mutare Methodist Center. Harare, Zimbabwe, August, 1989.

Kodzai, William, Headmaster of secondary school. Harare, July, 1989.

Mabvuta, Benjamin, teacher, George Stark Secondary School. Harare, August 2, 1989.

Mazaiwana, Edward, former teacher and inspector of schools, member of the Judges Commission, 1962. Harare, Zimbabwe. August, 1989.

Musumhi, Eliott, Education Officer. Harare, July, 1989.

Muzorewa, Abel, bishop of the United Methodist Church in Zimbabwe since 1968, former president of the African National Council, and interim prime minister of Zimbabwe in 1979. Harare, July 27, 1983.

Sithole, Ndabaningi, founder member of the African National Congress (1957), former president of ZANU, and former member of the transitional government (1979). Harare, Zimbabwe, July 22, 1983.

Smith, Ian D., prime minister from April 13, 1964, to March 3, 1979, and president of the Rhodesia Front Party from 1964 to 1979. Harare, Zimbabwe, July 20, 1983.

Name Index

Subject Index

About the Author

DICKSON A. MUNGAZI is Professor in the Center for Excellence in Education at Northern Arizona University.